PHARMACOLOGY - RESEARCH, SAFETY TESTING AND REGULATION

SECURING THE PHARMACEUTICAL SUPPLY CHAIN

ISSUES AND PERSPECTIVES

PHARMACOLOGY - RESEARCH, SAFETY TESTING AND REGULATION

Additional books in this series can be found on Nova's website under the Series tab.

Additional e-books in this series can be found on Nova's website under the e-book tab.

PHARMACOLOGY - RESEARCH, SAFETY TESTING AND REGULATION

SECURING THE PHARMACEUTICAL SUPPLY CHAIN

ISSUES AND PERSPECTIVES

LENORA WHITE
EDITOR

NOVINKA
New York

Library of Congress Cataloging-in-Publication Data

ISBN: 978-1-63463-448-9

Published by Nova Science Publishers, Inc. † New York

CONTENTS

Preface		**vii**
Chapter 1	Pharmaceutical Supply Chain Security *Susan Thaul*	**1**
Chapter 2	Statement of Janet Woodcock, Director, Center for Drug Evaluation and Research, FDA. Hearing on "Securing Our Nation's Prescription Drug Supply Chain"	**27**
Chapter 3	Testimony of Elizabeth A. Gallenagh, Vice President, Government Affairs, Healthcare Distribution Management Association. Hearing on "Securing Our Nation's Prescription Drug Supply Chain"	**33**
Chapter 4	Testimony of Christine Simmon, Senior Vice President, Policy & Strategic Alliances, Generic Pharmaceutical Association. Hearing on "Securing Our Nation's Prescription Drug Supply Chain"	**37**
Chapter 5	Testimony of Michael Rose, Vice President, Supply Chain Visibility, Johnson and Johnson Health Care Systems, Inc. Hearing on "Securing Our Nation's Prescription Drug Supply Chain"	**45**

Chapter 6	Testimony of Tim Davis, Owner, Beaver Health Mart Pharmacy. Hearing on "Securing Our Nation's Prescription Drug Supply Chain"	**49**
Chapter 7	Testimony of Allan Coukell, Director, Medical Programs, The Pew Charitable Trusts. Hearing on "Securing Our Nation's Prescription Drug Supply Chain"	**53**
Chapter 8	Testimony of Carmen A. Catizone, Executive Director, National Association of Boards of Pharmacy. Hearing on "Securing Our Nation's Prescription Drug Supply Chain"	**61**
Chapter 9	Statement of Deborah M. Autor, Deputy Commissioner for Global Regulatory Operations and Policy, FDA. Hearing on "Securing The Pharmaceutical Supply Chain"	**67**
Chapter 10	Drug Safety: FDA Faces Challenges Overseeing the Foreign Drug Manufacturing Supply Chain. Statement of Marcia Crosse, Director, Health Care, U.S. Government Accountability Office. Hearing on "Securing the Pharmaceutical Supply Chain"	**77**
Index		**93**

PREFACE

The drug package that a community pharmacist hands to a patient, or a hospital pharmacist sends to a patient's bedside, or a physician administers in the medical office has reached the end of a complicated path. That path is called a supply or distribution chain. The upstream portion of the chain includes the journey of each active and inactive ingredient and their chemical components to the manufacturer that creates the finished drug product. The downstream chain, which this report addresses, includes the repackagers, wholesale distributors, associated storage and transport companies, and, finally, the dispenser.

Dispensers include independent community or chain pharmacies, hospitals or other health care facilities, and physicians' offices. Usually the supply chain provides consumers with unadulterated prescription drugs. However, the chain is potentially vulnerable, and when it breaks, a dispenser might provide a counterfeit product containing no active ingredient, less-than-labeled dosage, or a dangerous substitution. The dispenser might also provide a mishandled or diverted drug that has become sub- or superpotent or has gone past its expiration Usually the supply chain provides consumers with unadulterated prescription drugs.

However, the chain is potentially vulnerable, and when it breaks, a dispenser might provide a counterfeit product containing no active ingredient, less-than-labeled dosage, or a dangerous substitution. The dispenser might also provide a mishandled or diverted drug that has become sub- or superpotent or has gone past its expiration. This book serves as a primer on pharmaceutical supply chain issues. It describes the chain from manufacturer to patient, including where it is vulnerable; summarizes current federal law, regulation, and FDA policies that Congress and the agency designed to protect the integrity of the final drug product, and indicates where those protections may falter; notes state-level and professional association activities; and discusses areas that Congress, FDA, and industry, health care, and patient stakeholders have suggested might be changed to increase the security of the pharmaceutical supply chain.

Chapter 1 - This report serves as a primer on pharmaceutical supply chain issues. It (1) describes the chain from manufacturer to patient, including where it is vulnerable; (2) summarizes current federal law, regulation, and FDA policies that Congress and the agency designed to protect the integrity of the final drug product, and indicates where those protections may falter; (3) notes state-level and professional association activities; and (4) discusses areas that Congress, FDA, and industry, health care, and patient stakeholders have suggested might be changed to increase the security of the pharmaceutical supply chain.

Chapter 2 - This is the Statement of Janet Woodcock, Director, Center for Drug Evaluation and Research, FDA.

Chapter 3 - This is the Testimony of Elizabeth A. Gallenagh, Vice President, Government Affairs, Healthcare Distribution Management Association.

Chapter 4 - This is the Testimony of Christine Simmon, Senior Vice President, Policy & Strategic Alliances, Generic Pharmaceutical Association.

Chapter 5 - This is the Testimony of Michael Rose, Vice President, Supply Chain Visibility, Johnson and Johnson Health Care Systems, Inc.

Chapter 6 - This is the Testimony of Tim Davis, Owner, Beaver Health Mart Pharmacy.

Chapter 7 - This is the Testimony of Allan Coukell, Director, Medical Programs, The Pew Charitable Trusts.

Chapter 8 - This is the Testimony of Carmen A. Catizone, Executive Director, National Association of Boards of Pharmacy.

Chapter 9 - This is the Statement of Deborah M. Autor, Deputy Commissioner for Global Regulatory Operations and Policy, FDA.

Chapter 10 - This is the Drug Safety: FDA Faces Challenges Overseeing the Foreign Drug Manufacturing Supply Chain. Statement of Marcia Crosse, Director, Health Care, U.S. Government Accountability Office.

In: Securing the Pharmaceutical Supply Chain ISBN: 978-1-63463-448-9
Editor: Lenora White

Chapter 1

PHARMACEUTICAL SUPPLY CHAIN SECURITY*

Susan Thaul

SUMMARY

The drug package that a community pharmacist hands to a patient, or a hospital pharmacist sends to a patient's bedside, or a physician administers in the medical office has reached the end of a complicated path. That path is called a supply or distribution chain. The upstream portion of the chain includes the journey of each active and inactive ingredient and their chemical components to the manufacturer that creates the finished drug product. The downstream chain, which this report addresses, includes the repackagers, wholesale distributors, associated storage and transport companies, and, finally, the dispenser. Dispensers include independent community or chain pharmacies, hospitals or other health care facilities, and physicians' offices.

Usually the supply chain provides consumers with unadulterated prescription drugs. However, the chain is potentially vulnerable, and when it breaks, a dispenser might provide a counterfeit product containing no active ingredient, less-than-labeled dosage, or a dangerous substitution. The dispenser might also provide a mishandled or diverted drug that has become sub- or superpotent or has gone past its expiration

* This is an edited, reformatted and augmented version of a Congressional Research Service publication R43106, prepared for Members and Committees of Congress, dated October 31, 2013.

date. In addition to the potential harm to patients, these security breaches can affect a manufacturer's reputation and financial bottom line.

Congress has addressed pharmaceutical supply chain security several times over the past 107 years. The 1906 Food and Drugs Act focused on labeling; the 1938 Federal Food, Drug, and Cosmetics Act (FFDCA) addressed adulteration, misbranding, and the registration and inspection of manufacturing establishments; and the Prescription Drug Marketing Act (PDMA, P.L. 100- 293) required that wholesale distributors be licensed by the states and required that a wholesale distributor, except one in a specified ongoing relationship with the manufacturer, provide to the purchasing distributor or dispenser a statement—called a pedigree—"identifying each prior sale, purchase, or trade of such drug." More recently, the Food and Drug Administration Amendments Act of 2007 (FDAAA, P.L. 110-85) required the Secretary to "develop standards and identify and validate effective technologies for the purpose of securing the drug supply chain against counterfeit, diverted, subpotent, substandard, adulterated, misbranded, or expired drugs"; and, in 2012, the Food and Drug Administration Safety and Innovation Act (FDASIA, P.L. 112-144) expanded registration and reporting requirements. Despite current federal law and actions by state legislatures, opportunities for breaches of the supply chain continue to exist. The 112th and 113th Congresses have worked to craft a set of national requirements that would protect both patient and manufacturer, and allow the assignment of accountability for identified problems, while attempting to manage cost and avoiding a confusing patchwork of state legislation.

In their work, House and Senate policymakers have been considering many decisions. These include, for example, definitions; pedigrees; track-and-trace technologies; serialization; lot- and unit-level requirements; authentication; interoperable data collection and systems; data confidentiality and access; requirements for transaction reporting and notification regarding suspect deliveries; implementation timing; licensure, registration, and accreditation standards for entities in the supply chain; accountability; cost; and the relationship between federal and state laws. After passing individual bills (H.R. 1919 and S. 959), majority and minority leadership of the House Committee on Energy and Commerce and the Senate Committee on Health, Education, Labor, and Pensions announced an agreement on September 25, 2013. The House passed the text of the agreement, H.R. 3204, on September 28, 2013, and the bill awaits Senate action.

PHARMACEUTICAL SUPPLY CHAIN: WHY PEOPLE CARE

The prescription drug that you picked up on the way to work this morning may have changed hands many times before the pharmacy clerk handed you the amber vial with its sticker label and perhaps one or two multi-page information inserts about the drug. That means that there were many potential opportunities for your drug to be mishandled or even substituted with a counterfeit. The counterfeit could be a watered down version of the actual drug, a sugar-filled non-medicinal fake, or a substitute chemical that looks, weighs, and reacts like the real drug but is actually toxic. While, overall, the U.S. drug supply is typically safe, Congress, the Food and Drug Administration (FDA), industry groups, and consumers are working to devise a system to limit opportunities for counterfeiting and mishandling.

Health experts call the drug's journey a *supply chain*. It begins with the ingredients a manufacturer uses, carries through the manufacturing process, and continues through the distribution system of wholesalers, warehouses, and transportation to the dispensing retail and institutional pharmacies—all the way to you, the consumer, the patient.[1] FDA, a federal scientific regulatory agency within the Department of Health and Human Services (HHS), regulates not only which drugs manufacturers may sell in the United States but also the integrity of the drugs through the supply chain, which is now global.[2]

In April 2013 testimony before the House Committee on Energy and Commerce, Janet Woodcock, the Director of FDA's Center for Drug Evaluation and Research, described the chain as follows.[3]

> [T]he increasingly complex drug supply chain, from raw source materials to finished products for consumers, presents multiple opportunities for the product to be contaminated, diverted, or otherwise adulterated. Our efforts to secure the supply chain include minimizing risks that arise anywhere along the supply chain continuum, from sourcing a product's ingredients through the overseeing of a product's manufacture, storage, transit, sale, and distribution. A breach at any point in this continuum could lead to dangerous and even deadly outcomes for patients.

Dr. Woodcock referred to problems "including contamination, diversion, counterfeiting, and other adulteration."[4] She gave several examples of counterfeit and stolen or diverted products: counterfeit Adderall and Vicodin sold on the Internet; stolen insulin vials needing refrigeration that were later purchased by patients without accountability for appropriate handling; and a stolen and expired seizure drug that "made it back into the legitimate supply chain and was being returned for credit."[5]

Additional examples of specific breaks in the supply chain include human growth hormone bought from Medicaid patients and sold by a Florida wholesaler in 2008;[6] insulin cargo stolen in 2009 that appeared among drugs sold by three wholesalers;[7] and, in 2010, a licensed Texas wholesaler offering prescription drugs obtained from patients.[8] Other publicized breaches of the supply chain have involved "fraudulent versions" of Botox "sold by unlicensed suppliers who are not part of the legitimate U.S. supply chain";[9] counterfeit Lipitor that U.S. consumers purchased from United Kingdom sources;[10] and counterfeit Avastin (with no active ingredient) that some U.S. medical practices bought from foreign distributors.[11]

This report serves as a primer on pharmaceutical supply chain issues.[12] It (1) describes the chain from manufacturer[13] to patient, including where it is vulnerable; (2) summarizes current federal law, regulation, and FDA policies that Congress and the agency designed to protect the integrity of the final drug product, and indicates where those protections may falter; (3) notes state-level and professional association activities; and (4) discusses areas that Congress, FDA, and industry, health care, and patient stakeholders have suggested might be changed to increase the security of the pharmaceutical supply chain.

Pharmaceutical Supply Chain: How It Works

To understand how the supply chain functions, it helps to know the extent of FDA's involvement with prescription drug safety and effectiveness. FDA regulates the approval, production, distribution, and advertising of prescription drugs.[14] It works to prevent unsafe, ineffective, subpotent, superpotent, or adulterated drugs from reaching pharmacies and patients in the United States—whether introduced on purpose or inadvertently.[15]

Before FDA approves a manufacturer's application to sell a prescription drug, it requires, among other things, that a manufacturer demonstrate that its product is safe and effective for its intended use, that directions on the label are clear and appropriate, and that the drug will be manufactured in specific production lines that have been registered and approved by FDA. *After FDA approves* the application, the manufacturer must continue production according to FDA-approved "good manufacturing practices" (GMPs).[16] The manufacturer must register each establishment involved in drug production with FDA and provide a list of current products,[17] and periodically open its production facilities to FDA inspection.

After production, the manufacturer typically sends, perhaps via a repackager, the drug to FDA-registered U.S. drug wholesale distributors (authorized distributors of record, secondary wholesale distributors, and others) for further distribution. Industry observers estimate that "consumers receive 11 million prescriptions per day from more than 150,000 locations throughout the US. Our drug distribution network involves tens of thousands of independent companies."[18] States license or authorize the pharmacists and wholesalers who sell and distribute pharmaceuticals within their borders and also license the physicians and dentists who prescribe the drugs.

As illustrated in *Figure 1*, many entities are part of the downstream pharmaceutical supply chain. Definitions of the players vary somewhat across federal and state laws and regulations and across proposed federal systems.[19] The following textbox provides general descriptions.

Participants in Drug Supply Chain

A *manufacturer* produces the drug product and is usually the entity that submits the application to FDA for approval to market the product or that holds the approval. A *wholesale distributor* sells the drug to "persons other than a consumer or patient" (21 CFR 203.3).

A *primary wholesale distributor* gets the drug products directly from the manufacturer and sells them to other wholesalers or dispensers. Three large primary wholesale distributors accounted for 85% of U.S. pharmaceutical wholesaling revenue; these are McKesson Corp., Cardinal Health Inc., and AmerisourceBergen Corp.[20]

An *authorized distributor of record (ADR)* is a wholesale distributor that has a relationship with a manufacturer that is ongoing, defined in regulations as including a written agreement specifying which products it will distribute and for which time period (21 CFR 203.3). Not all primary wholesalers are ADRs.

The term *secondary wholesale distributor* generally applies to wholesale distributors that acquire drug products from a wholesale distributor, not directly from the manufacturer. Some wholesale distributors focus on a region of the United States; others focus on a specialty market, say, of cancer drugs, or on the discounted drug market.[21]

A *repackager* removes a drug from its container and places in in another, usually smaller, container for sale to a distributor or dispenser.[22]

A *third-party logistics provider* may take temporary physical possession of the drug, such as during transport or warehousing, under contract with a manufacturer, distributor, or dispenser, but does not assume ownership of the drug.

A *dispenser* provides the drug to the consumer/patient. A dispenser may be an independent, community pharmacy; a retail chain pharmacy; a hospital or health care facility; a doctor's office; etc.

In addition to the members of the supply chain, others have an interest in its functioning. The primary *federal regulator* of drug safety, and therefore the drug supply chain, is the Food and Drug Administration (FDA), joined by others, such as the Centers for Disease Control and Prevention (CDC) and the Federal Trade Commission (FTC), as warranted. A *state regulator* can be a board of pharmacy, often placed within a state department of health. *Professional and industry organizations* with interest in pharmaceutical supply chain security include those representing pharmacists, pharmacies, health care institutions, manufacturers, distributors and wholesalers, and data- and code-based technology (hardware and software) developers and maintainers.[23]

Figure 1 presents the steps a finished drug product may take on its way from the manufacturer (labeled A) to the dispenser (labeled D) who will give the drug to the individual patient. This segment of the supply path is called *downstream*. The *upstream* segment ends with the manufacturer and involves the sources of materials that the manufacturer uses to produce the finished drug product, such as active pharmaceutical ingredients and inactive ingredients (e.g., fillers, binders, and colors).

A manufacturer may sell directly to a dispenser, but usually sells to a primary wholesale distributor (labeled B). The primary wholesale distributor may sell directly to a dispenser or may sell to a secondary wholesale distributor (labeled C) who sells it to the dispenser. A dispenser may return unopened and unexpired medication to the wholesaler who may then sell it to another dispenser or to another wholesaler or return it to the manufacturer. The combinations are numerous. Interspersed throughout the chain may be third-party logistics providers who transport or warehouse the drug under contract to the manufacturer, distributor, or dispenser.

At each change of hands, the drug could be vulnerable to theft, mishandling, adulteration, and tampering;[24] for example, part of a legitimate shipment may be stolen for resale elsewhere and substituted with a fake. Problems may arise at other times; for example, an otherwise legitimate shipment may be inadequately refrigerated in a truck or warehouse. The colored lines in *Figure 1* illustrate alternate paths from manufacturer to patient.

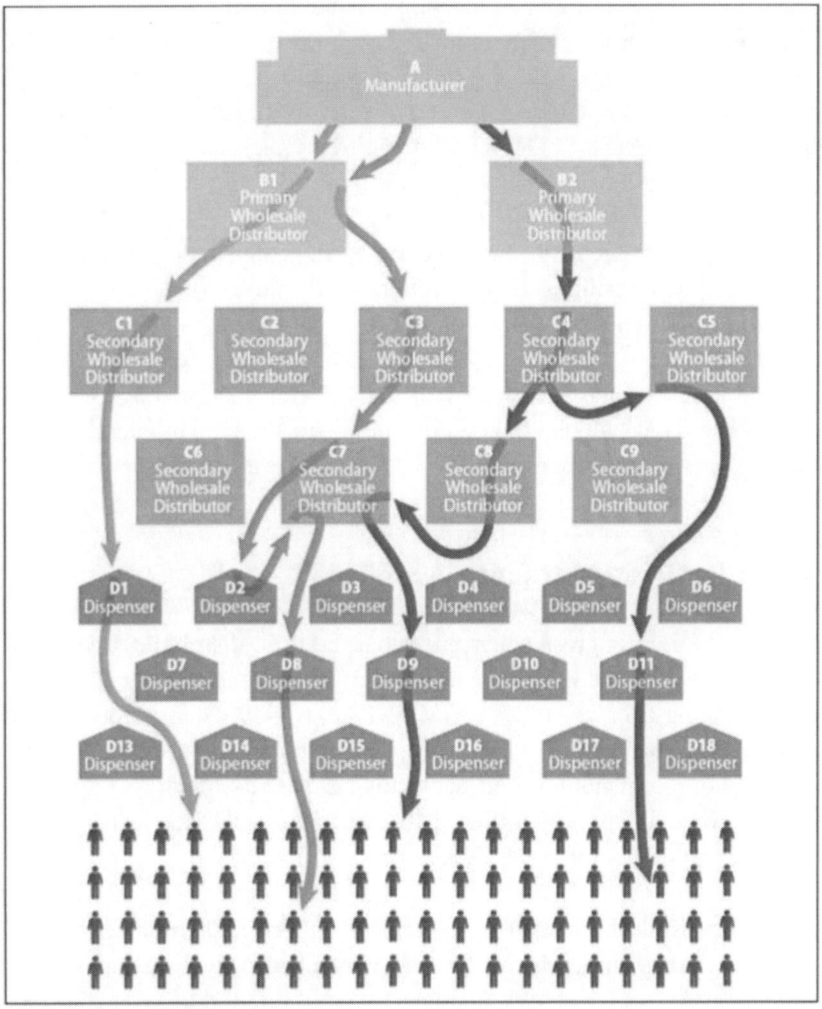

Source: Prepared by CRS.

Figure 1. Downstream Pharmaceutical Supply Chain. (for illustration).

How Congress Has Moved to Regulate the Supply Chain

FDA's earliest authorities, in 1906, concerned product integrity. Subsequent changes in the law related to product integrity and safety reflected the mid-century pharmaceutical industry with mostly domestic factories. Since its passage in 1938, the Federal Food, Drug, and Cosmetic Act (FFDCA), as amended, both directly addresses and indirectly influences the pharmaceutical supply chain. Relevant FFDCA sections cover topics including prohibitions and penalties regarding adulterated or misbranded drugs (e.g., Sections 301, 303, 501, and 502),

pharmaceutical security (e.g., Section 505D), registration and inspection of producers and facilities (e.g., Sections 510 and 704), and imports and exports (e.g., Section 801), among others.

In the last quarter century, Congress has made three focused attempts at improving supply chain security by amending the FFDCA. Each one added tools—standards, penalties, required planning—to strengthen federal oversight of the supply chain, as described below. Gaps, however, remain.

Prescription Drug Marketing Act of 1987

In the 1980s, Congress determined that the drug distribution system was not sufficiently "closed" to prevent abuse of drug samples. The Prescription Drug Marketing Act of 1987 (PDMA, P.L. 100-293)[25] amended FFDCA Section 503. It banned the sale, trade, and purchase of drug samples, and mandated storage, handling, and accounting standards for drug samples. By adding a new Subsection 503(e), PDMA also addressed other segments of the supply chain with the following changes to the FFDCA:

- required that wholesalers, except for authorized distributors of record, provide to the recipient "a statement ... identifying each prior sale, purchase, or trade of such drug.... ," often referred to as a pedigree;
- required each manufacturer to maintain a current list of its authorized distributors of record;
- stated that no one may engage in wholesale distribution unless licensed by a state in accordance with the Secretary's guidelines;

- required the Secretary[26] to issue guidelines, by regulation, establishing minimum standards for wholesaler licensing to include storage and handling and records;
- and defined *authorized distributor of record (ADR)* and *wholesale distribution* (see earlier textbox).

PDMA also established civil and criminal penalties for violations of its provisions.

Implementation of FFDCA Section 503(e)—in particular the first bullet, above—has not gone smoothly. To enforce the law, the FDA drafted regulations that would require drug companies to maintain a detailed "chain of custody" (also known as a pedigree) for every pharmaceutical product sold in this country.[27] The recorded pedigree would allow manufacturers to trace back suspected counterfeit shipments. FFDCA Section 503(e)(1)(A) [21 U.S.C. 353(e)(1)(A)] states:[28]

> Each person who is engaged in the wholesale distribution of a drug subject to subsection (b) of this section [a prescription drug] and who is not the manufacturer or an authorized distributor of record of such drug shall, before each wholesale distribution of such drug (including each distribution to an authorized distributor of record or to a retail pharmacy), provide to the person who receives the drug a statement (in such form and containing such information as the Secretary may require) identifying each prior sale, purchase, or trade of such drug (including the date of the transaction and the names and addresses of all parties to the transaction).

However, the law specifically excluded manufacturers' authorized distributors of record (ADRs) from this pedigree requirement. Because ADRs sell most drugs into secondary drug wholesale distribution markets, the PDMA recordkeeping requirement created a dilemma. Because the law does not require that a manufacture or an ADR give the records or pedigree with the drugs, the secondary distributors do not necessarily have the chain-of-custody information that the law requires them to provide to their customers.

For that reason, when FDA published final regulations to implement this section of the PDMA in December 1999,[29] the Small Business Administration petitioned the agency, arguing that enforcement of the provision would drive 4,000 or more secondary distributors out of business. Subsequently, FDA delayed the effective date of this provision's enforcement repeatedly,[30] most recently because it believed that industry voluntary conversion to an electronic pedigree was imminent, in which case the rule would be superfluous. In

November 2006, FDA announced the availability of a compliance policy guide (CPG 160.900) regarding the December 1, 2006, implementation of its PDMA pedigree regulations (21 CFR 203.3(u) and 203.50)), along with a guidance for industry to answer questions about PDMA requirements.[31] One week later, a court issued a preliminary injunction to prohibit FDA's implementing key pieces of the rule and FDA published an addendum to its guidance for industry, describing the injunction's effect on various elements of the regulatory requirements.[32] In March 2010, FDA stated that, "As a result of this litigation, FDA has been exercising its enforcement discretion concerning the drug pedigree requirements and only requiring that drug pedigrees go back to the last 'authorized distributor of record.'"[33] In July 2011, FDA issued a proposed rule to remove its rule on pedigree requirements for wholesale distribution (21 CFR 203.50(a)).[34]

Food and Drug Administration Amendments Act of 2007

The PDMA chain-of-custody requirements are not the only provisions in the FFDCA that address the security of the pharmaceutical supply chain.

With the FDA Amendments Act of 2007 (FDAAA, P.L. 110-85), Congress added FFDCA Section 505D [21 U.S.C. 355d] "Pharmaceutical Security."[35] The law directed the Secretary to "develop standards and identify and validate effective technologies for the purpose of securing the drug supply chain against counterfeit, diverted, subpotent, substandard, adulterated, misbranded, or expired drugs." In particular, the law required the Secretary to

> develop a standardized numerical identifier (which, to the extent practicable, shall be harmonized with international consensus standards for such an identifier) to be applied to a prescription drug at the point of manufacturing and repackaging (in which case the numerical identifier shall be linked to the numerical identifier applied at the point of manufacturing) at the package or pallet level, sufficient to facilitate the identification, validation, authentication, and tracking and tracing of the prescription drug.

Complying with that requirement, FDA issued "Draft Guidance for Industry on Standards for Securing the Drug Supply Chain—Standardized Numerical Identification for Prescription Drug Packages" in January 2009.[36] The agency issued the final guidance in March 2010.[37] Note that FDAAA did not authorize the Secretary to *require* the use of SNIs. Action on use of an SNI will likely depend on future legislation.

FDAAA also directed the Secretary to undertake other activities. They fall into three general areas: addressing promising technologies, such as radiofrequency identification technology, nanotechnology, encryption technologies, and other track-and-trace technologies; undertaking enhanced and joint enforcement activities with other federal and state agencies; and establishing regional capabilities for validation and inspection.[38]

Food and Drug Administration Safety and Innovation Act of 2012

Five years after FDAAA, attempts by Congress, FDA, and other stakeholders to craft a comprehensive supply chain plan culminated in the Food and Drug Administration Safety and Innovation Act (FDASIA, P.L. 112-144). Members, committees, bipartisan and bicameral staff groups, and stakeholder groups had released several bills and discussion drafts in the 112th Congress in advance of FDASIA.[39]

Although all parties expressed willingness to compromise because of the urgent need to find solutions to security threats and the complications that would arise if each state went its own way with laws and regulations, they were unable to agree on a complete approach.

FDASIA, as enacted, expanded FDA authority regarding manufacturer registration, facility inspection, and importation.[40] It included provisions to allow FDA to refuse entry of an imported drug if the manufacturing facility inspection was denied or limited; enhance penalties for suppliers of counterfeit or substandard products; and require a unique manufacturing facility identifier for both domestic and foreign facilities. (The following textbox provides a longer summary of the FDAAA drug supply chain provisions.)

FDASIA Drug Supply Chain Provisions[41]

In general, Title VII, Drug Supply Chain:

- Expanded the registration information required from the owners or operators of domestic and foreign drug establishments to include a unique facility identifier and information about importers.

- Expanded registration information required to include establishments that manufacture excipients (such as fillers, preservatives, and flavors) for listed products.
- Required the Secretary to maintain an electronic database of unique facility identifiers.
- Required the Secretary to carry out manufacturing establishment inspections according to a risk-based schedule for both prescription and nonprescription drugs; specified risk factors and required reports.
- Required manufacturers to submit required records in advance or in lieu of inspections within a reasonable timeframe; and required the Secretary to sufficiently describe the records requested and to provide receipt confirmations.
- Required that a drug be deemed adulterated if the owner or operator of a facility used in its manufacture delays, denies, or limits an inspection, or refuses to permit entry or inspection.
- Allowed the Secretary to destroy an adulterated, misbranded, or counterfeit drug offered for import if it is valued at $2,500 or less; and included language about notice, storage, cost liability, and regulations.
- Expanded the Secretary's authority to administratively detain a product found to be adulterated or misbranded during a facility inspection to include drugs (prior authority was for device and tobacco products).
- Allowed the Secretary to, in specified conditions, keep confidential the information relating to drug inspections that a foreign government provided voluntarily.
- Noted that, with respect to the criteria for deeming a drug to be adulterated, "current good manufacturing practices" include quality controls in manufacturing, and assurance of the safety of raw materials.
- Allowed the Secretary to enter into agreements with foreign governments to recognize inspections of foreign establishments in specified situations.
- Allowed the Secretary to require, as a condition of granting a drug admission to the United States, an importer to provide specified information demonstrating that the drug complies with requirements of this act.

- Required a commercial importer to register with the Secretary and submit, among other things, a unique facility identifier; required the Secretary to promulgate regulations to establish good importer practices; and prohibited the importation of drugs by unregistered commercial importers.
- Allowed the Secretary to require that a registered manufacturer, a wholesaler, or a distributor (other than for retail sale) notify the Secretary when that person knows (1) that the use of a drug may result in serious illness or death; (2) of a significant theft of such drug; or (3) of the counterfeiting of such drug that is in U.S. commerce or could be imported.
- Required imprisonment for up to 20 years or a fine up to $1 million for a person who knowingly and intentionally adulterates a drug so that the drug has a reasonable probability of causing serious adverse health consequences or death to humans or animals.
- Added trafficking in a counterfeit drug to the list of violations subject to fines and imprisonment under the U.S. criminal and penal code, and directed the U.S. Sentencing Commission to amend guidelines to increase penalties to reflect the serious nature of these offenses.
- Asserted U.S. authority to enforce the FFDCA for a violation that occurs outside the United States if the product was intended for U.S. import or if an act committed in the United States furthers the violation.

Although FDASIA included several elements of a broader plan, key items, such as chain-ofcustody documentation and track-and-trace technologies, remained unresolved. Following FDASIA passage, Members and staff continued discussions, attempting to find an effective and feasible mix would cover domestic and foreign facilities.[42]

STATE ACTIVITY

In the absence of a federal plan, about half of all states have passed their own laws to address drug pedigrees and supply chain security.[43] Legislation is pending in some other states. The approaches and extent of law and regulation vary by state, but they generally address similar issues such as definitions, licensing, permits, registration, pedigrees, and recordkeeping, among other topics.

In discussing federal proposals for a uniform national system, Members of Congress as well as stakeholders testifying at congressional hearings often refer to the law that California first passed in 2004 and then amended (regarding implementation dates) in 2006 and 2008.[44] The California law now calls for its pedigree requirements to go into effect in 2015.

Central to the California law is a required electronic pedigree to include every transaction from the manufacturer to the dispenser of the prescription drug.[45] The pedigree is to include information about the seller (e.g., identifying information and registration number), the drug (e.g., name, quantity, dose, expiration date, lot numbers, and a unique identification number), and the shipment (e.g., size and number of containers, and invoice number). The pedigree data must be handled in a system that is interoperable, "ensuring compatibility throughout all states of distribution." The law provides definitions and exemptions (e.g., medical gases and drugs for veterinary use). One provision of the California law[46] is particularly relevant for federal policymakers:

> Upon the effective date of federal legislation or adoption of a federal regulation addressing pedigree or serialization measures for dangerous drugs, Sections ... shall become inoperative.

Members of Congress who want a comprehensive supply chain law (such as what California has enacted) may not want to pass a less extensive federal law because it could prevent California from implementing its pedigree requirements. Some manufacturers and distributors have cautioned that not only are the California requirements expensive but they rely on technologies that are not fully formed. Others report that the technologies are sufficiently advanced and they have already begun gearing up to comply with the California law.

PROFESSIONAL AND INDUSTRY ASSOCIATION ACTIVITY

Several associations and ad hoc alliances of industry participants recommended supply chain security systems or proposed legislation that they could support.

The *National Association of Boards of Pharmacy* (NABP) has worked with states to create a Model State Pharmacy Act and Model Rules.[47] The 2010 Model Act defines *wholesale distributor*[48] and recommends the adoption of *electronic pedigrees* subject to the availability of adequate technology.

NABP has also developed criteria and a process to accredit distributors. NABP's website describes its Verified-Accredited Wholesale Distributors (VAWD) program, established in 2004 and updated in May 2013, and notes that 21 states recognize VAWD, including 3 that require it.[49] NABP describes the VAWD program as follows:

> Wholesale distributers that display the VAWD Seal as part of their accreditation have undergone a criteria compliance review, including a rigorous review of their operating policies and procedures, licensure verification, survey of facility and operations, background checks, and screening through the NABP Clearinghouse. Accredited facilities are reviewed annually and undergo a site survey every three years.

The *Pharmaceutical Distribution Security Alliance (PDSA)* issued draft legislative language in February 2012: the Pharmaceutical Traceability Enhancement Code (RxTEC) Act.[50] The draft would create a comprehensive system involving a machine-readable graphic on individual packages to support lot-level tracing of a product to its immediate previous and subsequent owners. The system would be implemented incrementally, with manufacturer, repackager, wholesale distributor, and dispenser requirements beginning three, four, five, and six years, respectively, after enactment.

POLICY DECISION POINTS

Versions of pharmaceutical supply chain legislation have been considered in both the House and Senate in the 113th Congress.[51] This report is designed as a backgrounder for those new to the issue, thus it does not track current legislation.

All parties to the discussion agree to one big-picture goal: pharmaceutical supply chain security. Several sub-goals, some of them overlapping, are evident in current and prior legislative proposals that would

- *protect the patient* from ineffective or dangerous drugs that may be in the supply chain as a result of counterfeiting, theft and resale, or manufacturing, transportation, or storage mishaps;
- *protect the manufacturer*, who can lose both money and reputation if its product harms a patient, regardless of whether the fault laid with the manufacturer's actions; and
- *allow* the assignment of accountability for identified problems. In working toward those subgoals, policymakers are also trying to
- *avoid* having to comply with *diverse state requirements* by enacting a national plan; and
- establish a system that is logistically *feasible at manageable cost.*

Although Congress, FDA, and affected industry and health care stakeholders agree on an overall goal (increasing supply chain security), they have disagreed about approaches and details. The drafters and negotiators of legislative language face many policy decision points. Some policy decision points involve *whether to do* something at all (e.g., Is the current system of state regulation better than proposed federal changes?). Others would involve the implementation *timing* of a requirement (e.g., implement six months or 10 years after enactment, study and consider recommendations six months or 10 years after enactment, or implement in clearly defined action and timing stages); or the *scope* of a requirement (e.g., types of drugs, types of facilities, time period covered, timing of activity).

The following section lays out many of the terms and policy decision points under discussion by Members, committees, and staff of Congress. Each paragraph presents a term (e.g., track and trace) under discussion and a very brief suggestion of how it fits into the overall attempt to regulate the pharmaceutical supply chain.

Definitions. Different industries, professions, and statutes use similar terms differently.[52] In creating legislation for pharmaceutical supply chain security, policymakers must decide how to define the meaning of terms they use. For example, wholesaler, distributor, third-party logistics provider, manufacturer, pharmacy, package, and pedigree.[53]

Pedigree. A description of the drug (possibly information such as name, amount, dosage, manufacturer, lot number) and a statement of the transaction history of the drug, including each transfer of ownership (and/or physical possession) of the product. This could include seller, purchaser, amount transferred, lot numbers, among other information. Current movement is away from paper toward an electronic pedigree.

Track and trace. A system that involves electronically tagging each package with a unique identifier (serialization), noting each transfer of a drug package, and maintaining a database of all such transactions.[54] For example, a manufacturer might want to track a package to facilitate a recall if a problem were noted. A public health authority (or the manufacturer) might want to trace back to where a package has been to determine the source of a local problem.

Serialization (SNI—standardized numerical identifier). A mark placed on a package at the manufacturing facility (and again at the time of repackaging) that is unique to that package. As FDAAA required, the Secretary has developed a standardized numerical identifier (SNI). FFDCA, including FDAAA amendments, does not give the Secretary authority to require the use of SNIs.

Lot- or unit-level activity. Whether a labeling or tracking requirement applies at the level of the lot or the unit. A lot is the full output of a manufacturer's production run; it can include thousands of units. A unit is the smallest package that is delivered to the dispenser (retail or hospital pharmacy or clinical setting) who will dispense it to a patient. The use of unit-level tracking and tracing could allow quicker and more focused recalls and real-time investigation of adverse events. This more extensive approach would also be more expensive. Some proposals would separate the labeling task from the reporting task in setting implementation goals or requirements.

Supply chain. Analysts speak of the *upstream* supply chain (sources and path of ingredients that go to the manufacturer) and the *downstream* supply chain (path of the finished product after it leaves the manufacturer). Current legislative discussions are focused on the downstream chain. For each requirement regarding pedigrees/transaction records, authentication/verification, and other supply chain security activities, legislation could specify start and end points; however, opinions differ on which points to use.[55] The most inclusive (and with higher up-front costs for supply-chain participants) would cover all transactions beginning with the manufacturer and ending with retail sale to the patient.

Authentication. When accepting a shipment, the recipient (e.g., distributor, warehouse, or dispenser) could be required to verify the SNI and the distribution history.

Technology choice. Under a track-and-trace system, an SNI would be applied at the manufacturer or repackager level to each package. Information about contents and its distribution path could be included or linked. Analysts debate the benefits and limitations of various technologies such as two-dimensional bar codes or radio-frequency identification (RFID) for track and trace purposes. Further, the technologies are evolving as packaging and data management engineers are designing other systems for supply chain use.

Interoperability. For a track and trace system to work as envisioned, the data maintained by the manufacturer and each subsequent link in the chain must have compatible formats and definitions. Interoperability would also apply to the way data are communicated (e.g., a standardized language) and interpreted by those contributing to or using the data.

Data management. In a track-and-trace system, some entity would maintain standards on how participants collect, store, protect, and use data. Such management could be centralized or decentralized (distributed), each approach having benefits and limitations.[56]

Data access. Policymakers could specify in legislation several choices regarding data access— such as who would have access to which data elements—or leave it to the responsible agency (most likely FDA) to establish by regulation and guidance. Considerations might include for what purposes someone might use the data; and whether the user would need real-time data to track an unknown contaminant or could use semi-annual records for reports.

Confidentiality. Decisions about data management and access could involve consideration of the confidentiality of information about patients, dispensers, clinicians, and business entities across the supply chain.

Notification. Distributors or dispensers may find that a shipment includes suspected or confirmed counterfeit or substandard drug products. A new law might require that they notify other supply chain participants. The law or subsequent regulations could direct how the data management group or the overseeing federal agency could manage that information.

Penalties. Legislation could specify whether penalties (civil and/or criminal) would apply to various violations of compliance with provisions relating to, for example, labeling or completing transaction records. FFDCA already allows penalties for, among other violations, acts of counterfeiting, misbranding, and marketing of unapproved drugs.

Implementation timing. Various legislative proposals set different time frames for each step—for example, use of SNI, lot-level transaction reporting, unit-level transaction reporting, and issuance of proposed and final regulations.

Licensure, registration, and accreditation. In general, states choose whether and how to license members of professions and specific activities. At the federal level, FDA requires entities to register with FDA if they participate in specified activities; for example, a manufacturer of a drug in commercial distribution.[57] Some legislative proposals address the federal role in licensing standards for wholesale distributors and other members of the supply chain.

Accountability. Registration of supply chain participants would support assigning or accepting accountability for errors, accidents, and weaknesses along the chain. How a supply chain security system is structured could affect how foreign participants engage with the recordkeeping and how FDA could manage oversight and enforcement of compliance.[58]

Cost. Consideration of cost is often a part of decisions regarding scope, implementation dates, reporting requirements, and other elements of a supply chain security system. Issues raised include who bears the cost (e.g., manufacturer, patient, government, distributors, dispensers); what the cost would be given current technology and systems; and what it might be if new products are developed in response to new requirements.

Federal and state jurisdiction. There seems to be general agreement that a uniform set of national standards has advantages over a patchwork of varying state requirements. However, the requirements in federal legislation might *preempt* state law and regulation. Those who favor the more extensive requirements that some states (such as California) have enacted would prefer that federal requirements be a floor upon which states could choose to build.

CONCLUDING COMMENTS

As drug production has shifted to a global supply chain of manufacturers, processers, packagers, importers, and distributors,[59] FDA leadership, among others, has suggested that the agency's current statutory authority does not match its responsibilities to ensure that the nation's drug supply is secure.[60] In April 2013, FDA's Dr. Woodcock testified,[61]

> A robust track-and-trace system, in which each drug produced would be tracked as it passes through the distribution system and allows purchasers to verify its distribution history, would improve the ability to identify and detect potentially harmful products if they enter the supply chain. Another potential benefit would be to improve the efficiency of product recalls. Imagine a system that enables the distributor or pharmacist to readily determine if they have sold or now have in stock a drug that had been identified as a counterfeit or subject to a recall. They could quickly remove that product from the supply chain, keeping the patient out of harm's way. The only way this can be done effectively is if

all supply chain stakeholders participate in the system and if all legitimate products have a way to be identified and tracked as they are distributed from the point of manufacture.

Many Members of the current Congress have been trying, as had their predecessors, to craft legislation that could help (1) keep counterfeit, mishandled, and substandard drugs away from patients; (2) maintain clear lines of accountability; (3) use appropriate levels of technology and data management; and (4) avoid unintentional adverse effects on patients, industry, communication systems, and relationships of all with each other and the states and FDA. Current[62] congressional attention is on H.R. 3204, the Drug Quality and Security Act, the text of which was released as an agreement by majority and majority leadership of the Senate Committee on Health, Education, Labor, and Pensions and the House Committee on Energy and Commerce on September 25, 2013. Title II is the proposed Drug Supply Chain Security Act. The House passed H.R. 3204 on September 28, 2013. The bill now awaits Senate action.

End Notes

[1] Because the term consumer could refer to retail or hospital pharmacy or clinician's practice that purchases the drug from a distributor or the manufacturer in addition to the person who uses the drug, this report uses the term patient to refer to the person who uses the drug.

[2] Statement of Deborah M. Autor, Deputy Commissioner for Global Regulatory Operations and Policy, Food and Drug Administration, Department of Health and Human Services, before the Committee on Health, Education, Labor, and Pensions, United States Senate, September 14, 2011, http://www.fda.gov/NewsEvents/Testimony/ucm271073.htm.

[3] Statement of Janet Woodcock, Director, Center for Drug Evaluation and Research, Food and Drug Administration, Department of Health and Human Services, before the Subcommittee on Health, Committee on Energy and Commerce, U.S. House of Representatives, hearing on "Securing Our Nation's Prescription Drug Supply Chain," April 25, 2013, http://www.fda.gov/ NewsEvents/Testimony/ucm349186.htm.

[4] Ibid.

[5] Ibid.

[6] FDA Office of Criminal Investigations, link to Department of Justice June 4, 2009 press release, http://www.fda.gov/ ICECI/CriminalInvestigations/ucm277094.htm.

[7] Statement of Deborah M. Autor, Deputy Commissioner for Global Regulatory Operations and Policy, Food and Drug Administration, Department of Health and Human Services, before the Committee on Health, Education, Labor, and Pensions, United States Senate, September 14, 2011, http://www.fda.gov/NewsEvents/Testimony/ucm271073.htm; and FDA, "Update to FDA Alert About Stolen Insulin," August 26, 2009, http://www.fda.gov/ForConsumers/ ConsumerUpdates/ucm180320.htm.

[8] FDA Office of Criminal Investigations, link to Department of Justice March 18, 2010 press release, http://www.fda.gov/ICECI/CriminalInvestigations/ucm271770.htm.

[9] FDA, "Fraudulent Versions of Botox Found in the United States," Drug Safety and Availability, April 26, 2013, http://www.fda.gov/Drugs/DrugSafety/ucm349503.htm.

[10] FDA, "Counterfeit 'Lipitor' Sold in the United Kingdom," Safety Alerts for Human Medical Products, August 2, 2005, http://www.fda.gov/Safety/MedWatch/SafetyInformation/Safety AlertsforHumanMedicalProducts/ ucm151056.htm.

[11] FDA, "Counterfeit Version of Avastin in U.S. Distribution," Drug Alerts and Statements, February 14, 2012, http://www.fda.gov/Drugs/DrugSafety/ucm291960.htm.

[12] Other sources that provide background information include FDA, "FDA Counterfeit Drug Task Force Reports," http://www.fda.gov/Drugs/DrugSafety/ucm169825.htm; Government Accountability Office (GAO), "Food and Drug Administration: Response to Heparin Contamination Helped Protect Public Health; Controls That Were Needed for Working With External Entities Were Recently Added," GAO-11-95, October 29, 2010; Pew Health Group, "After Heparin: Protecting Consumers from the Risks of Substandard and Counterfeit Drugs," July 12, 2011, http://prescriptionproject.org/after_heparin_report/; Institute of Medicine (IOM), Countering the Problem of Falsified and Substandard Drugs, Gillian J. Buckley and Lawrence O. Gostin, editors, Washington DC: National Academies Press, 2013;

[13] This report focuses on the downstream supply chain—from the manufacturer to the consumer. The upstream supply chain involves the paths of the active and inactive ingredients and their processing that occur before the manufacturer creates the finished product.

[14] FDA also regulates the safety and effectiveness of animal drugs. This report addresses only the human drug supply chain.

[15] For a fuller discussion, see CRS Report R41983, How FDA Approves Drugs and Regulates Their Safety and Effectiveness, by Susan Thaul.

[16] See, for example, FDA, "Current Good Manufacturing Practices (cGMP) for Drugs: Reports, Guidances and Additional Information," Page Last Updated: 10/07/2010, http://www.fda.gov/Drugs/DevelopmentApprovalProcess/ Manufacturing/QuestionsandAnswersonCurrentGoodManufacturingPracticescGMPforDrugs/default.htm; FDA, "Questions and Answers on Current Good Manufacturing Practices (CGMP) for Drugs," Page Last Updated: 12/20/2012, http://www.fda.gov/Drugs/ DevelopmentApprovalProcess/Manufacturing/ucm124740.htm.

[17] FDA, "Drug Registration and Listing System (DRLS & eDRLS)," Page Last Updated: 04/12/2013, http://www.fda.gov/Drugs/GuidanceComplianceRegulatoryInformation/Drug RegistrationandListing/ucm2007058.htm.

[18] Adam Fein, "Securing America's Pharmaceutical Supply Chain," Drug Channels blog, May 15, 2008, http://www.drugchannels.net/2008/05/my-op-ed-securing-supply-chain.html, printed in Pharmalot blog, May 13, 2008, http://www.pharmalot.com/2008/05/the-op-ed-securing-the-supply-chain/.

[19] FDA, "The Prescription Drug Marketing Act: Report to Congress," 2001, http://www.global compliance.com/pdf /Prescription%20Drug%20Marketing%20Act%20(PDMA)%20Report%20to%20Congress.pdf); 21 CFR 201.1, 203.3, 208.3, 314.3; Healthcare Distribution Management Association (HDMA), "HDMA Fact Sheet on PDMA," Copyright 2010, http://www.healthcaredistri bution.org/press_room/pdma_facts.asp; National Coalition of Pharmaceutical Distributors (NCPD), "Position paper of the National Coalition of Pharmaceutical Distributors (NCPD)," http://www.ncpdusa.org/pdf/NCPD_Position_Paper_Final_020107.pdf; and

Modern Distribution Management (MDM), "2010 MDM Market Leaders: Top 10 Pharmaceutical Wholesalers," May 27, 2010, http://www.mdm.com/ 2010-mdm-market-leaders-top-10-pharmaceutical-wholesalers/PARAMS/article/26126.

[20] See Pew Health Group, "After Heparin: Protecting Consumers from the Risks of Substandard and Counterfeit Drugs," July 12, 2011, http://prescriptionproject.org/after_heparin_report/; and Adam Fein, "Trends and top distributors in the pharmaceuticals sector," in MDM Market Leaders 2012: Top Pharmaceuticals Distributors, 2013, http://www.mdm.com/2012-mdm-market-leaders-top-pharmaceuticals-distributors.

[21] There were about 2,000 secondary distributors in 2007 (Pew Health Group, "After Heparin: Protecting Consumers from the Risks of Substandard and Counterfeit Drugs," July 12, 2011, http://prescriptionproject.org/ after_heparin_report/; and FDA, "The Prescription Drug Marketing Act: Report to Congress," June 2001, http://www.fda.gov/downloads/ RegulatoryInformation/Legislation/FederalFoodDrugandCosmeticActFDCAct/ SignificantAmendmentstotheFDCAct/PrescriptionDrugMarketingActof1987/UCM203186. pdf.

[22] U.S. Pharmacopeia, <1146> Packaging Practice—Repackaging a Single Solid Oral Drug Product into a Unit-Dose Container," http://www.pharmacopeia.cn/v29240/usp29nf24s 0_c1146.html; and Florida Department of Business and Professional Regulation, "Prescription Drug Repackager," http://www.myfloridalicense.com/dbpr/ddc/ Prescription DrugRepackager.html.

[23] Examples include the American Pharmacists Association (APhA), American Society of Health-System Pharmacists (ASHP), Biotechnology Industry Organization (BIO), Generic Pharmaceutical Association (GPhA), Health Industry Distributors Association (HIDA), Healthcare Compliance Packaging Council (HCPC), Healthcare Distribution Management Association (HDMA), National Association of Boards of Pharmacy (NABP), National Association of Chain Drug Stores (NACDS), National Community Pharmacists Association (NCPA), Pharmaceutical Distribution Security Alliance (PDSA), and Pharmaceutical Research and Manufacturers of America (PhRMA).

[24] Statement of Deborah M. Autor, Deputy Commissioner for Global Regulatory Operations and Policy, Food and Drug Administration, Department of Health and Human Services, before the Committee on Health, Education, Labor, and Pensions, United States Senate, September 14, 2011, http://www.fda.gov/NewsEvents/Testimony/ucm271073.htm.

[25] U.S. Congress, House Committee on Energy and Commerce, Prescription Drug Marketing Act of 1987, H.Rept. 100- 76, 100th Cong., 1st Sess. Washington, GPO, April 30, 1987, p. 7. Congress amended and clarified some PDMA provisions in the Prescription Drug Amendments (PDA) of 1992, P.L. 102-353.

[26] In this report, the Secretary means the Secretary of Health and Human Services.

[27] By imposing strict recordkeeping requirements, FDA hoped, among other things, to ensure the safety and quality of all drugs that are exported and later imported back into the country (FDA, "The Prescription Drug Marketing Act: Report to Congress," 2001, http://www. globalcompliance.com/pdf/ Prescription%20Drug%20Marketing%20Act%20(PDMA)%20Report%20to%20Congress.p df); and 21 CFR part 203 (Prescription Drug Marketing).

[28] FFDCA Section 503(e); and H.Rept. 100-76 [to accompany H.R. 1207], Mr. Dingell, April 30, 1987.

[29] FDA had previously issued a guidance letter in August 1988 (Attachment E to FDA, "Prescription Drug Marketing Act Report to Congress," June 2001, http://www.fda.gov/ downloads/RegulatoryInformation/Legislation/

FederalFoodDrugandCosmeticActFDCAct/SignificantAmendmentstotheFDCAct/ PrescriptionDrugMarketingActof1987/UCM203186.pdf, see PDF pages 50-65) and a proposed rule in March 1994 (FDA, "21 CFR Parts 203 and 205 [Docket No. 92N-0297] RIN 0905-AC81, Prescription Drug Marketing Act of 1987; Prescription Drug Amendments of 1992; Policies, Requirements, and Administrative Procedures; Proposed rule," Federal Register, vol. 59, No. 49, March 14, 1994, http://www.gpo.gov/fdsys/pkg/FR-1994-03-14/html/94-5540.htm).

[30] FDA, "Prescription Drug Marketing Act of 1987; Prescription Drug Amendments of 1992; Policies, Requirements, and Administrative Procedures; Delay of Effective Date," Federal Register, February 23, 2004 (21 CFR 203). For PDMA history, see http://www.fda.gov/ oc/pdma/report2001/report.html, p. 7.

[31] FDA, "Prescription Drug Marketing Act Pedigree Requirements under 21 CFR Part 203 Compliance Guide and Guidance for Industry: Prescription Drug Marketing Act Pedigree Requirements Questions and Answers; Notice of availability of guidances," Federal Register, vol. 71, no. 220, November 15, 2006, pp. 66448-66450, http://www.gpo.gov/ fdsys/pkg/FR-2006-11-15/pdf/06-9211.pdf; FDA, "Compliance Policy Guide (CPG) 160.900 Prescription Drug Marketing Act—Pedigree Requirements under 21 CFR Part 203," November 2006, http://www.fda.gov/ICECI/ComplianceManuals/ Compliance PolicyGuidanceManual/ucm073857.htm; and FDA, "Prescription Drug Marketing Act (PDMA) Requirements: Questions and Answers," Center for Drug Evaluation and Research, Office of the Commissioner, Office of Regulatory Affairs, November 2006, http://www.fda.gov/downloads/Drugs/GuidanceComplianceRegulatoryInformation/Guidances/UCM134399.pdf.

[32] FDA, "Addendum to FDA's 'Guidance for Industry: PDMA Pedigree Requirements—Questions and Answers' Related to the Preliminary Injunction ordered 12/5/06 in RxUSA Wholesalers, Inc. v. HHS," December 15, 2006, http://www.fda.gov/downloads/Drugs/ GuidanceComplianceRegulatoryInformation/Guidances/UCM134399.pdf.

[33] FDA, "Chapter 2. FDA Authority," Regulatory Procedures Manual, March 2010, http://www.fda.gov/downloads/ICECI/ComplianceManuals/RegulatoryProceduresManual/ UCM074340.pdf.

[34] In the Federal Register notice, FDA wrote, "We note that even with the removal of § 203.50(a), the pedigree requirements of section 503(e)(1)(A) of the FD&C Act would still be in effect" (FDA, "[Docket No. FDA–2011–N– 0446] Removal of Certain Requirements Related to the Prescription Drug Marketing Act; Opportunity for Public Comment; Proposed rule," Federal Register, vol. 76, no. 135, July 14, 2011, pp. 41434-41438, http://www.gpo.gov/ fdsys/pkg/FR-2011-07-14/pdf/2011-17696.pdf). Later, FDA noted that the case (RxUSA Wholesale, Inc. v. HHS) had ended and proposed withdrawing Section. 203.50(a) (Federal Register, vol. 77, no. 29, February 13, 2012, p. 7949).

[35] For the pharmaceutical security and other provisions in FDAAA, see CRS Report RL34465, FDA Amendments Act of 2007 (P.L. 110-85), by Susan Thaul.

[36] Federal Register, v. 74, no. 11, January 16, 2009, pp. 3054-3055.

[37] FDA, "Guidance for Industry: Standards for Securing the Drug Supply Chain—Standardized Numerical Identification for Prescription Drug Packages," Office of the Commissioner, Center for Drug Evaluation and Research, Center for Biologics Evaluation and Research, and Office of Regulatory Affairs, March 2010, http://www.fda.gov/ downloads/Regulatory Information/Guidances/UCM206075.pdf.

[38] For more information on supply chain technologies, see, for example, Lisa A Daigle, "Following Pharmaceutical Products Through the Supply Chain," ASHP (American Society

of Health-System Pharmacists] Policy Analysis, August 2012, http://www.ashp.org/DocLibrary/Advocacy/AnalysisPaper/Following-Pharmaceutical-Products.aspx; and materials from a February 2011 FDA public workshop, "Determination of System Attributes for the Tracking and Tracing of Prescription Drugs," http://www.fda.gov/downloads/Drugs/NewsEvents/UCM245540.pdf.

[39] Legislative attempts in the 112th Congress included, for example, H.R. 1483 (Representatives Dingell, Waxman, Pallone, and DeGette); H.R. 3026 (Representatives Matheson and Bilbray); a March 16, 2012 discussion draft (Senators Bennet and Burr); RxTEC (a February 2012 draft from the Pharmaceutical Distribution Security Alliance (PDSA)); S. 3187 (§722 as passed by Senate); and several proposals discussed during FDASIA negotiations.

[40] For more detail on the supply chain and other provisions of FDASIA, see CRS Report R42680, The Food and Drug Administration Safety and Innovation Act (FDASIA, P.L. 112-144), coordinated by Susan Thaul. To compare the House- and Senate-passed versions of the bills, see CRS Report R42564, FDA User Fees and the Regulation of Drugs, Biologics, and Devices: Comparative Analysis of S. 3187 and H.R. 5651, coordinated by Susan Thaul.

[41] The drug supply chain provisions in Title VII of FDASIA amended FFDCA Sections 301, 303, 304, 501, 502, 510, 704, 708, 801; added new FFDCA Sections 568 and 809; and amended 18 U.S.C. 2320.

[42] "As Congress Continues to Mull Track and Trace, California Plows Ahead on ePedigree," Drug Industry Daily, August 3, 2012.

[43] Two 2011 reports by the National Alliance for Model State Drug Laws (NAMSDL) described pedigree-related statutes in 20 states and regulations in 16 states (NAMSDL, "Drug Pedigree Requirements for Pharmacies and Wholesalers: State Statutes," July 2011, http://www.namsdl.org/documents/StateStatutoryCompilationJuly2011.pdf; and NAMSDL, "Drug Pedigree Requirements for Pharmacies and Wholesalers: State Regulations," July 2011, http://www.namsdl.org/documents/StateRegulatoryCompilationJuly2011.pdf). According to 2013 testimony from the Healthcare Distribution Management Association (HDMA), 29 states have laws or regulations that go "beyond the federal PDMA standards" (Testimony of Elizabeth A. Gallenagh, Vice President, Government Affairs and General Counsel, Healthcare Distribution Management Association, before the House Energy and Commerce Committee, Subcommittee on Health, April 25, 2013, http://www.healthcare distribution.org/testimony/2013-04- 25_gallenagh_testimony.pdf).

[44] California Department of Consumer Affairs, Board of Pharmacy, "California E-Pedigree Law," http://www.pharmacy.ca.gov/about/e_pedigree_laws.shtml. This webpage has links to "Background and Summary of E-Pedigree Laws," California Business and Professions Code sections, PowerPoint "Overview of the Law, questions and answers document, and text of the law.

[45] The actual language in the California pedigree provision refers to a "dangerous drug." However, elsewhere in the California code that term is defined to mean a prescription drug.

[46] California Board of Pharmacy, "Section 4034.1. Enactment of Federal Pedigree Legislation," 2013 Lawbook for Pharmacy, http://www.pharmacy.ca.gov/laws_regs/lawbook.pdf.

[47] National Association of Boards of Pharmacy (NABP), "Model State Pharmacy Act and Model Rules of the National Association of Boards of Pharmacy," August 2010, http://www.nabp.net/publications/model-act.

[48] NABP's Model Act defines wholesale distributor as "including but not limited to Manufacturers, Repackagers, own-label distributors, private-label distributors, jobbers, brokers, warehouses, including Manufacturers' and Distributors' warehouses, Co-licensees,

Exclusive Distributors, Third-Party Logistics Providers, Chain Pharmacy Warehouses, and Wholesale Drug warehouses, independent Wholesale Drug traders, and retail Pharmacies that conduct Wholesale Distributions" (National Association of Boards of Pharmacy (NABP), "Model State Pharmacy Act and Model Rules of the National Association of Boards of Pharmacy," August 2010, http://www.nabp.net/publications/model-act).

[49] NABP, "VAWD [Verified-Accredited Wholesale Distributors]," 2013, http://www.nabp.net/programs/accreditation/ vawd; and NABP, "NABP Updates VAWD Criteria, Continuing Efforts to Help Secure the Integrity of US Drug Supply Chain for the Protection of Public Health," May 8, 2013, http://www.nabp.net/news/nabp-updates-vawdcriteria-continuing-efforts-to-help-secure-the-integrity-of-us-drug-supply-chain-for-the-protection-of-public-health—2.

[50] Pharmaceutical Distribution Security Alliance (PDSA), "Pharmaceutical Traceability Enhancement Code (RxTEC) Act," February 27, 2012 Discussion Draft; link to summary is available on the Health Industry Distributors Association (HIDA) website at http://www.hida.org.

[51] After posting two discussion drafts, the House Committee on Energy and Commerce reported a bill that the House passed on June 3, 2013: H.R. 1919, the Safeguarding America's Pharmaceuticals Act of 2013. The Senate Committee on Health, Education, Labor, and Pensions, after posting a discussion draft, voted to favorably report S. 957, the Drug Supply Chain Security Act.

[52] A February 2013 report from the Institute of Medicine (IOM) begins with a discussion of "the competing and often overlapping definitions of the terms counterfeit, falsified, and substandard" and how different usage in legal and public health contexts can muddy policy discussions (IOM, Countering the Problem of Falsified and Substandard Drugs, Gillian J. Buckley and Lawrence O. Gostin, editors, Washington DC: National Academies Press, 2013).

[53] In layman vocabulary, for example, the term package could apply to any of the following deliveries: the package the patient picks up at the drug store with, for example, 30 tablets; or the package of 100 bottles each with 250 tablets that the secondary distributor delivers to the drug store; or the package with 1000 of the 250-tablet bottles or 500 cartons each with four 2000-tablet jugs. If the legislative language does not clearly define what package means when it requires something at the package level (e.g., a standardized numerical identifier, tracking and tracing to the package level within a certain amount of time), that ambiguity may cause problems in implementation.

[54] See, for example, Pew Health Group, "After Heparin: Protecting Consumers from the Risks of Substandard and Counterfeit Drugs," July 12, 2011, http://prescriptionproject.org/after_heparin_report/; and FDA, "The Prescription Drug Marketing Act: Report to Congress," June 2001, http://www.fda.gov/downloads/RegulatoryInformation/ Legislation/ FederalFoodDrugandCosmeticActFDCAct/SignificantAmendmentstotheFDCAct/ PrescriptionDrugMarketingActof1987/UCM203186.pdf.

[55] Questions include whether to require a retail pharmacy or a hospital pharmacy to track what it dispenses in addition to what it receives. Obstacles include the need for scanners and staff time (see, for example, Lisa Daigle, "Following Pharmaceutical Products Through the Supply Chain," American Society of Health-System Pharmacists (ASHP) Policy Analysis, August 2012, http://www.ashp.org/DocLibrary/Advocacy/AnalysisPaper/Following-PharmaceuticalProducts.aspx).

[56] FDA held a public workshop, "Determination of System Attributes for the Tracking and Tracing of Prescription Drugs," in February 2011, Links to the agenda, discussion topics,

PowerPoint slides, and workshop summary are at http://www.fda.gov/ Drugs/ NewsEvents/ucm239382.htm. Introductory material referred to the need for "standardized practices in data format, data communications, and data interpretation" (FDA, "FDA Track and Trace Public Workshop," February 15-16, 2011, slide 23, http://www. fda.gov/ downloads/Drugs/NewsEvents/UCM245540.pdf.

[57] 21 CFR Part 207—Registration of Producers of Drugs and Listing of Drugs in Commercial Distribution.

[58] Pew Health Group, "After Heparin: Protecting Consumers from the Risks of Substandard and Counterfeit Drugs," July 12, 2011, http://prescriptionproject.org/after_heparin_report/.

[59] See, for example, FDA, "A Special Report: Pathway to Global Product Safety and Quality," July 2011, http://www.fda.gov/downloads/AboutFDA/CentersOffices/OC/Global Product Pathway/UCM262528.pdf; and Pew Health Group, "After Heparin: Protecting Consumers from the Risks of Substandard and Counterfeit Drugs," July 12, 2011, http://prescription project.org/after_heparin_report/.

[60] Statement of Deborah M. Autor, Deputy Commissioner for Global Regulatory Operations and Policy, FDA, before the Senate Committee on Health, Education, Labor, and Pensions, "Securing the Pharmaceutical Supply Chain," September 14, 2011, http://www.fda.gov/ NewsEvents/Testimony/ucm271073.htm; and statement of Janet Woodcock, Director, FDA Center for Drug Evaluation and Research, before the Subcommittee on Oversight and Investigations, House Committee on Energy and Commerce, "FDA's Ongoing Heparin Investigation," April 29, 2008, http://www.fda.gov/NewsEvents/ Testimony /ucm115242. htm.

[61] Statement of Janet Woodcock, Director, Center for Drug Evaluation and Research, Food and Drug Administration, Department of Health and Human Services, before the Subcommittee on Health, Committee on Energy and Commerce, U.S. House of Representatives, hearing on "Securing Our Nation's Prescription Drug Supply Chain," April 25, 2013, http://www.fda.gov/NewsEvents/Testimony/ucm349186.htm.

[62] Earlier in the 113th Congress, the House Committee on Energy and Commerce and the full House passed H.R. 1919, the Safeguarding America's Pharmaceutical's Act, and the Senate Committee on Health, Education, Labor, and Pensions reported S. 959, the Pharmaceutical Quality, Security, and Accountability Act.

In: Securing the Pharmaceutical Supply Chain ISBN: 978-1-63463-448-9
Editor: Lenora White

Chapter 2

STATEMENT OF JANET WOODCOCK, DIRECTOR, CENTER FOR DRUG EVALUATION AND RESEARCH, FDA. HEARING ON "SECURING OUR NATION'S PRESCRIPTION DRUG SUPPLY CHAIN"*

INTRODUCTION

Mr. Chairman, Ranking Member Pallone and Members of the Subcommittee, I am Dr. Janet Woodcock, Director of the Center for Drug Evaluation and Research (CDER) at the Food and Drug Administration (FDA or the Agency), which is part of the Department of Health and Human Services (HHS). Thank you for the opportunity to be here today to discuss the important issue of securing the supply chain for prescription drug products.

Securing the Supply Chain for Prescription Drugs

As FDA has previously testified before this Committee, the increasingly complex drug supply chain, from raw source materials to finished products for consumers, presents multiple opportunities for the product to be contaminated, diverted, or otherwise adulterated. Our efforts to secure the supply chain

* This is an edited, reformatted and augmented version of a statement presented April 25, 2013 before the House Committee on Energy and Commerce, Subcommittee on Health.

include minimizing risks that arise anywhere along the supply chain continuum, from sourcing a product's ingredients through the overseeing of a product's manufacture, storage, transit, sale, and distribution. A breach at any point in this continuum could lead to dangerous and even deadly outcomes for patients.

In addition, we continue to see counterfeit drugs threaten American consumers' health. Counterfeit drugs raise significant public health concerns, because their safety and effectiveness are unknown. A counterfeit drug could contain a substance that is toxic to patients. But even a counterfeit drug with no active ingredient could prove harmful to patients who take it, thinking that they are taking a lifesaving or life-sustaining medication, when they are not. For example, in 2003, over $20 million in illegally imported and counterfeit Lipitor (atorvastatin calcium), a popular cholesterol-lowering drug, was distributed throughout the United States. The source and manufacturing methods of these drugs were unknown and therefore had the potential to endanger patients. As another example, in 2012, FDA learned of counterfeit versions of two controlled substances that were being sold on the Internet: Adderall (amphetamine aspartate), a drug used to treat attention deficit disorder, and Vicodin ES (acetaminophen; hydrocodone bitartrate), a drug used to treat pain. In both of these incidents, the counterfeits contained different active ingredients than the products they purported to be. Also in 2012, FDA alerted over 500 U.S. medical practices that they had purchased unapproved drugs, some of which may have included a counterfeit version of a cancer medicine. At least some of the counterfeit drugs contained no active ingredients. These examples are troubling because patients may not have received needed therapy or may have experienced harmful side effects.

Counterfeit drugs are not the only problem; stolen or diverted products also pose a threat to patients. Once products leave the legitimate supply chain, we have no idea how they are being stored or handled—or even if they have expired. When those drugs make their way back into the supply chain, they can pose a danger to patients. For example, in one case in 2009, approximately 129,000 vials of Levemir (insulin detemir) were stolen. Insulin is used to control blood sugar levels in patients with diabetes and should be stored in a refrigerator before use. A patient who received the stolen insulin had poor blood glucose control, likely as a result of it not being stored properly. In 2008, a shipment of Carbatrol (carbamazepine), a drug to treat seizures, was stolen while traveling from a company's manufacturing facility to its distribution center. The manufacturer reported that expired Carbatrol from the stolen lots made it back into the legitimate supply chain and was being returned for credit. In a case from 2011, a criminal diverted $2.7 million in prescription drugs by purchasing them from physicians who get discounted rates, and then reselling them to wholesalers at a profit. These diverted drugs included sterile injectable drugs, which usually require special storage and handling.

While we recognize that we may not be able to eliminate all problem products from the supply chain, we take every step we can to make the supply chain more secure to keep the illegitimate products out. Implementation of a system to fully track and trace prescription drugs throughout the supply chain would help in combating incidents like these counterfeit examples. In February 2013, the Institute of Medicine issued a report entitled "Countering the Problem of Falsified and Substandard Drugs," identifying a combination of actions that could reduce counterfeit and substandard drugs domestically and globally. The report recommends implementing a mandatory drug tracking system in the United States and recognizes how knowledge of where a product is and where it has been can greatly reduce the risks introduced by product diversion and porous supply chains.

A robust track-and-trace system, in which each drug produced would be tracked as it passes through the distribution system and allows purchasers to verify its distribution history, would improve the ability to identify and detect potentially harmful products if they enter the supply chain. Another potential benefit would be to improve the efficiency of product recalls. Imagine a system that enables the distributor or pharmacist to readily determine if they have sold or now have in stock a drug that had been identified as a counterfeit or subject to a recall. They could quickly remove that product from the supply chain, keeping the patient out of harm's way. The only way this can be done effectively is if all supply chain stakeholders participate in the system and if all legitimate products have a way to be identified and tracked as they are distributed from the point of manufacture.

FDA's Current Activities

The Food and Drug Administration Amendments Act of 2007 (FDAAA; Public Law 110-85) gave FDA authority to set standards for identification, validation, authentication, and tracking and tracing of prescription drugs; but, it did not provide the Agency with explicit authority to require an effective track-and-trace system for all drug products throughout the supply chain. In March 2010, FDA issued a final guidance for industry describing the Agency's current thinking for standardized numerical identification (also known as serialization) for prescription drug packages. This guidance was the first of several steps that FDA intends to take to implement these provisions of FDAAA. We held a Track-and-Trace Public Workshop in February 2011 to obtain public input on the necessary elements to achieve effective authentication and the desirable attributes of a track-and-trace system. FDA continues to work on developing these standards.

The Food and Drug Administration Safety and Innovation Act (FDASIA; Public Law 112-144) provided the Agency with new authorities that will help to secure the safety and integrity of drugs imported into, and sold in, the United States. For example, the law includes provisions that allow FDA to refuse admission of a product to the United States if inspection of the manufacturing facility is delayed, limited, or denied; require foreign and domestic companies to provide complete information on threats to the security of the drug supply chain; and improve current registration and listing information, making sure FDA has accurate and up-to-date information about foreign and domestic manufacturers. A robust track-and-trace system would complement these new authorities to further ensure that stolen, diverted, and counterfeit drugs do not enter the supply chain or are found more quickly if they do.

Next Steps

FDA has worked closely with Members of this Committee, your colleagues in the Senate, and other stakeholders to provide technical assistance in response to legislative proposals to secure the downstream pharmaceutical supply chain. Consistent with the position articulated by the President's Intellectual Property Enforcement Coordinator, FDA is focused on establishing an effective track-and-trace system. Broadly speaking, such a system should include:

- A clear path toward implementing an effective track-and-trace system to fully secure the supply chain and enhance protection of public health.
- Enforcement authority to ensure that parties adhere to implementation requirements.

- Requirements for all stakeholders to maintain the distribution history for drugs they handle, unless the system provides a way to verify a drug's authenticity and identify its complete history, when needed.
- Reasonable time frames for implementation based on what is technologically possible and what will result in the best possible outcome for public health.

CONCLUSION

An effective national track-and-trace system for all drug products throughout the supply chain would improve the security and integrity of the drug supply and ensure transparency and accountability of product distribution. Many of the challenges we have with securing the supply chain—including contamination, diversion, counterfeiting, and other adulteration—could be addressed by such a system. We look forward to continuing to work with the Committee to develop a system that meets this promise.

In: Securing the Pharmaceutical Supply Chain ISBN: 978-1-63463-448-9
Editor: Lenora White

Chapter 3

TESTIMONY OF ELIZABETH A. GALLENAGH, VICE PRESIDENT, GOVERNMENT AFFAIRS, HEALTHCARE DISTRIBUTION MANAGEMENT ASSOCIATION. HEARING ON "SECURING OUR NATION'S PRESCRIPTION DRUG SUPPLY CHAIN"*

Good morning Chairman Pitts, Ranking Member Pallone and Members of the Energy and Commerce Subcommittee on Health. I am Elizabeth Gallenagh, Vice President, Government Affairs and General Counsel for the Healthcare Distribution Management Association (HDMA). Thank you for the opportunity to inform the Subcommittee regarding the critically important issue of prescription drug pedigree and pharmaceutical supply chain safety. I also would like to thank Chairman Upton, Congressman Latta and Congressman Matheson for their leadership in this area.

HDMA represents the nation's primary pharmaceutical distributors that deliver more than nine million prescription drugs and other healthcare products every day to 200,000 pharmacy and provider settings across the country.

* This is an edited, reformatted and augmented version of testimony presented April 25, 2013 before the House Committee on Energy and Commerce, Subcommittee on Health.

Our 33 member companies purchase products from manufacturers and are responsible for storing, managing and delivering nearly 90 percent of all prescription medicines sold in the U.S. This critical public health function is performed with tremendous efficiency, resulting in nearly $42 billion in annual savings to the nation's healthcare system.

The pharmaceutical distribution industry's primary mission is to operate the safest, most secure and efficient supply chain in the world. As part of this mission, HDMA's members work to eliminate counterfeit and diverted medicines by capitalizing on the technological innovation and constant improvements in efficiency that are the foundation of our industry.

Today, I am here to express HDMA's strong support for a national, uniform approach to pedigree and the traceability of medicines throughout the supply chain. We support the core elements of the Latta-Matheson proposal and look forward to working with you and your Senate colleagues to enact federal legislation.

HDMA supports enhanced national wholesaler licensing standards and a new federal ceiling for pedigree and traceability requirements to improve safety and uniformity across the country, while establishing the foundation for longer-term electronic solutions, such as unit-level serialization and product tracing.

In addition to fundamentally addressing counterfeit and diverted medicines, a national approach to pedigree and traceability may be a useful tool in discouraging gray market activities associated with drug products in short supply. More importantly, it will put the U.S. on par with countries around the world engaging in serialization and traceability efforts.

After many years of debate, it appears that Congress finally may be poised to enact federal pedigree legislation. This is, in large part, due to a broad consensus among supply chain partners as well as growing support from Members of Congress and the leadership of Congressmen Latta and Matheson. While Congress, FDA and industry stakeholders have been working at this diligently for several years, it is critical that Congress act now due to the uncertainties faced by the industry, the need for uniformity across the supply chain and to ensure patient safety.

Because of the unique role HDMA members play in the supply chain between manufacturers and providers, they witness firsthand the complexities of dealing with the current 50-state patchwork of licensing and pedigree laws

Basic guidelines for pedigree were set forth nearly 25 years ago with the enactment of the federal Prescription Drug Marketing Act (PDMA). Since that time, activity at the state level has varied with some enacting complex electronic pedigree laws and others never going further than the original 1988 guidelines. Based on our experience, the complexities of dealing with multiple approaches in the states will only get worse if we fail to solve this problem now, at the national level.

Since Florida's first foray into raising pedigree and licensure requirements in 2003, we have seen dramatic variations across the country in both legislative activity and regulatory interpretation. This variation has occurred despite HDMA's attempts to work in every state along with fellow stakeholders and interested legislators and regulators to achieve more uniformity. Today, for example, 29 states have acted beyond the federal PDMA standards. The states of Florida and California are viewed as leaders in this arena. However, they take completely different approaches, with Florida considered to be the most stringent in terms of today's requirements, and California's law thought to be the most complex, with track-and-trace and electronic pedigree implementation beginning in 2015.

This patchwork not only creates operational challenges, but also leaves openings for bad actors to shop around for more lenient state rules — openings that could mean the difference between a fake or diverted medicine being dispensed or administered to an innocent patient in need of treatment. Because of this state-by-state variation, we believe that pedigree and traceability should be under the purview of Congress and the FDA.

HDMA has been a leader in this area, forming and participating in industry task forces and working groups that bring together manufacturers, distributors and pharmacies dedicated to identifying the operational and technical requirements for electronic pedigree, track-and-trace and traceability implementation. HDMA is also an active member of PDSA, the Pharmaceutical Distribution Security Alliance.

A comprehensive, practical approach would result in increased safety, continued efficiencies and minimal inconsistencies among competing state requirements — all of which will enable HDMA distributors and our supply chain partners to continue to deliver prescription drugs safely and efficiently every day.

HDMA commends Congressmen Latta and Matheson, along with the committee leadership, on continuing the dialogue and moving this effort forward with the release of the Latta-Matheson discussion draft. We believe that the framework of the draft is consistent with the basic foundation HDMA has supported through the years.

The bipartisan proposal includes the following core elements:

- National Uniformity

Adoption of national requirements for wholesaler licensing standards while preserving the states' ability to license and enforce, as well as uniform direct-purchase and standard pedigree (documentation of product transaction history) requirements. Taking this immediate first step will help to ensure the efficient flow of prescription drugs in interstate commerce, raise the bar for states that have not gone beyond the current federal PDMA "floor" and enhance protections for the most secure prescription drug supply chain in the world — further ensuring patient safety and access to lifesaving medicines.

- Unit-level Serialization

Currently, there is no mechanism required to identify a unique bottle of medicine. This proposal will require manufacturers to apply a unique identifier to prescription drugs at the unit and case levels. This would be the first in a series of steps designed to help protect the supply chain against counterfeit, adulterated or other substandard products by facilitating improved ability to identify non-legitimate items. Prescription drugs would be identified at the unit and case level with a serial number (SNI), lot number and expiration date.

- Data Exchange and Systems Development

Once product is serialized, it is believed that product traceability initially can be achieved at the lot level, with potential for traceability at more discrete levels as systems mature. As a result, exchange of transaction data will be possible and can be leveraged to provide additional efficiency and safety benefits within the supply chain. HDMA supports a migration toward traceability that includes deliberate, careful evaluation and assessment by FDA and stakeholders at each step.

There is no single element that will protect the supply chain from every threat but rather, a comprehensive solution should incorporate each of these elements.

We applaud the work that has been done to date and urge the Subcommittee to act on this important issue this year. Now is the time for Congress to act to bring cohesion and consistency to our national drug supply chain.

Thank you.

In: Securing the Pharmaceutical Supply Chain ISBN: 978-1-63463-448-9
Editor: Lenora White

Chapter 4

TESTIMONY OF CHRISTINE SIMMON, SENIOR VICE PRESIDENT, POLICY & STRATEGIC ALLIANCES, GENERIC PHARMACEUTICAL ASSOCIATION. HEARING ON "SECURING OUR NATION'S PRESCRIPTION DRUG SUPPLY CHAIN"*

Good morning Chairman Pitts, Ranking Member Pallone and Members of the House Energy and Commerce Subcommittee on Health. Thank you for inviting me to testify before the subcommittee on the important topic of securing our nation's pharmaceutical supply chain.

I am Christine Simmon, Senior Vice President, Policy & Strategic Alliances at the Generic Pharmaceutical Association. GPhA represents the manufacturers and distributors of finished dose generic pharmaceuticals, bulk pharmaceuticals and suppliers of other goods and services to the generic industry. Generic pharmaceuticals now fill 80 percent of all prescriptions dispensed in the United States, but account for only 27 percent of the total spending for prescription medicines. According to an analysis by IMS Health, the world's leading data source for pharmaceutical sales, the use of FDA-approved generic drugs in place of their brand counterparts has saved U.S. consumers, patients and the health care system more than $1 trillion over the past decade and $192.8 billion in 2011 alone — which equates to $1 billion in

* This is an edited, reformatted and augmented version of testimony presented April 25, 2013 before the House Committee on Energy and Commerce, Subcommittee on Health.

savings every other day. The quality and affordability of generic medicines is vital to public health and the sustainability of the health care system.

INTRODUCTION

For many years, GPhA has worked closely with multiple stakeholders across the supply chain to ensure that American consumers will continue to benefit from the safest and most secure prescription drug supply in the world. Both industry and the FDA are exceptionally vigilant against the distribution and sale of counterfeit and adulterated medicines.

Any presence of counterfeit and adulterated pharmaceuticals in our supply chain threatens both the health of patients and the integrity of our industry. As the makers of 80 percent of the prescriptions dispensed in the United States, the generic pharmaceutical industry is deeply committed to ensuring the security of our country's drug supply. GPhA believes that the problem of counterfeit medicines raises a significant public health concern that must be addressed systemically on a range of levels — from local to global, and throughout the drug supply chain.

Our commitment to this issue is further evidenced by our industry's strong support of last Congress' historic Generic Drug User Fee Act, which recognizes that while providing earlier access to effective medicines is critical — and the key aim of all other existing user fee programs — FDA's central mission is ensuring drug safety. We also applaud the efforts of this Committee in enacting the user fee program into law. The program holds all players, foreign or domestic, contributing to the U.S. generic drug system to the same Good Manufacturing Practices (GMP), and inspection standards, while expediting access to more affordable, high quality generic drugs; the generic drug user fee program also enhances FDA's ability to identify, track and require the registration of all contributors involved in each generic drug product sold in the U.S.

We also are members of the Pharmaceutical Distribution Security Alliance, or PDSA: a multi-stakeholder and interdisciplinary initiative whose membership spans the entire spectrum of the U.S. pharmaceutical distribution system, including manufacturers, wholesale distributors, third-party logistics providers and pharmacies.

The PDSA's mission is to develop, and help enact, a federal policy proposal that enhances the security and integrity of the domestic pharmaceutical distribution system for patients, and to articulate a technical migratory pathway to implement such a policy. The coalition's primary goal is to ensure patients have uninterrupted access to safe, authentic, FDA-approved medicine.

It is worth noting that low-cost generic drugs are rarely, if ever, targeted by counterfeiters. And in general, as the FDA acknowledges, "counterfeiting is quite rare within the U.S. drug distribution system." Nevertheless, the generic industry has been a leader in supporting numerous anti-counterfeiting efforts and developing methods to further protect the integrity of the pharmaceutical supply chain. The generic industry is committed to ensuring the safety of the millions of consumers nationwide who use safe, affordable generic medications. As such, we support a system built on the core principles of: a uniform, federal standard; technical requirements that support achievability; and a building-block approach to ensure an orderly implementation and avoid unintended consequences.

Last year, the effort to enact a national solution received strong support from key members in both the House and Senate but unfortunately was not enacted into law. We applaud this Committee for picking up where the previous effort left off, and we recognize and appreciate the dedicated attention to this issue given by Congressman Matheson and Congressman Latta.

UNIFORM FEDERAL STANDARD

As these efforts move forward, however, it is vital to ensure that any system is practical, focused, and uniform across the country. A uniform system founded on reliable technology and business practices would preclude the unintended consequence of erecting cost barriers to the distribution of safe and effective medicines.

For example, some anti-counterfeiting efforts, such as the drug pedigree model currently set to take effect in 2015 under California law, would require implementation of full electronic "track-and-trace" capabilities, where the entire distribution history, and the location, of every unit in the supply chain can be determined at any time. At present, the technology to support such a system is unreliable and underdeveloped, and the costs associated with such a model would be billions. Considering the myriad of manufacturers, packaging operations and potential exceptions, this is not a realistic expectation. An attempt to implement such a system would lead to confusion in the supply chain, aggravate product shortages and dramatically increase costs for all prescriptions, including generic medicines. The California law does include language providing for preemption of its requirements in the event that federal legislation is enacted, which we support.

ACHIEVABILITY

As the Committee begins its consideration of legislation to address this important issue, it is critical to understand how previous efforts at regulating the pharmaceutical supply chain — at both the state and federal level — have led us to where we stand today.

In 1988, Congress passed the Prescription Drug Marketing Act, or PDMA, requiring drugs to be tracked when they passed outside of the normal chain of distribution, which begins at the manufacturer, goes to authorized distributors and finally to the pharmacy. Congress found this necessary because the majority of drugs that were counterfeit, stolen, expired or obtained through fraud were handled by secondary wholesalers, who were not authorized to distribute a manufacturer's product. Manufacturers and their authorized distributors were exempted from these requirements, because the introduction of counterfeit medicines would rarely, if ever, occur in this link of the supply chain. However, the law was stayed by the FDA, and finally enjoined in 2006 by a federal district court in New York, in large part because the creation of a national drug tracking system including all supply chain participants had not been mandated, making the requirements potentially too difficult or impossible to fulfill for many legitimate distributors.

Since that time, this Committee and the Congress passed the Food and Drug Administration Amendments Act of 2007 (FDAAA), which directs the FDA to develop standards for the identification, validation, authentication and tracking of prescription drugs, as well as a standard numerical identifier to be applied to a prescription drug at the point of manufacturing and repackaging. While most of these standards have yet to be established, the FDA envisions a full track-and-trace system similar to that in California. We believe that the technology and processes necessary to achieve full track-and-trace are not fully mature at this time.

Additional federal legislation also has been introduced in recent years that would urge the establishment of national standards for an electronic tracking system. These proposals pursue the worthy goal of a single, uniform national standard for supply chain security, as opposed to a patchwork of differing state-by-state laws. However, the measures proposed would ultimately require an extensive track-and-trace model for each individual saleable unit of medicine that is simply unachievable within the proposed timeframes. GPhA believes that adoption of the California model, or one with very similar features, would raise the cost of medicine by billions of dollars over time, would be prone to error, and would have, at best, similar results to a less-expensive, more efficient model.

Building-Block Approach

GPhA recognized the shortcomings of the California-type approach early on and proposed its own alternative model in 2011 by publishing a white paper on an end-point authentication model. At that time, we began to work in PDSA with representatives from all sectors of the supply chain and helped create an industry consensus model that we believe makes large safety strides in incremental steps over time. We believe that a building-block approach enables the industry to achieve the necessary interoperability in achievable steps, all the while applying the knowledge and experience gained over time to refine the model. While our member companies are still reviewing the recently-released House draft, many elements of that draft are consistent with our proposed approach.

Specifically, as outlined in Phase I of the Latta-Matheson discussion draft, generic manufacturers have committed to identifying individual saleable units of medicine with labels, and maintaining and managing data in their systems that would associate the identifiers on individual bottles of medicine with the lot numbers of products. Verification that a specific unit was indeed identified by a manufacturer within a given production lot can provide information and security that is a major step forward from current practices. Unit-level identification provides greater granularity of a lot and improves the visibility of its distribution throughout the supply chain, and also provides unit-level data as an additional check. This system would help identify and prevent the introduction of suspect product through full lot traceability and allow regulatory authorities to validate the identifier of a product at the unit level.

And unlike a full track-and-trace system, which we do not believe is technologically feasible in the near term, the House language would provide immediate measures to increase supply chain security. The system established under the proposal will improve the efficiency and effectiveness of drug recalls and returns. In planning for the future, it would provide critical building blocks that can be expanded as public health threats, interoperability standards, and technologies evolve, and establish connectivity and infrastructure throughout the supply chain that will enable a variety of other capabilities and efficiencies. We also strongly support the e-labeling requirement in the discussion draft to provide more standardized, electronic prescription drug information that would increase patient safety and provide significant quality improvements and cost reductions to patients, manufacturers, prescribers and providers of pharmaceuticals by developing a more accurate, cost-effective and sustainable alternative to existing paper inserts. The discussion draft would also create more stringent federal standards and state licensing for wholesale distributors, and streamline requirements for manufacturers who also operate as distributors.

In keeping with many years of existing law, GPhA agrees with the Latta-Matheson discussion draft that intravenous (IV) products must be exempted from these regulations and urges that this exemption be maintained.

In short, the House proposal will replace the patchwork of inconsistent state laws, while increasing patient safety and enhancing our ability to identify and prevent the introduction of suspect products. It is important to recognize the limitations of technology and the necessity of other means of vigilance to address the issues of counterfeiting and diversion of drugs. There is no technology or tracking system that will stop all thieves and counterfeiters from attempting to divert products, or profit illegally.

GPhA supports the development of pilot programs to explore and evaluate methods to enhance the safety and security of the pharmaceutical distribution supply chain as well as the inclusion in the discussion draft of report mandates for the Government Accountability Office and Food and Drug Administration to assess implementation and pilot programs, respectively.

CONCLUSION

In conclusion, Mr. Chairman, GPhA and the industry share the concerns of the Committee with regard to maintaining the security of our country's drug supply and preventing the entry of counterfeit, diverted, stolen or other substandard medicines. The development of a uniform, national system is needed to give regulatory authorities another tool for enforcement, make it more difficult for criminals to breach the supply chain and enhance the ability of the supply chain to respond quickly when a breach has occurred. We believe the model proposed by the House includes many elements to achieve these goals. We look forward to working together with the House and Senate to develop a consensus measure on this important issue that can be enacted into law. Thank you and I would happy to answer any questions you may have.

In: Securing the Pharmaceutical Supply Chain ISBN: 978-1-63463-448-9
Editor: Lenora White

Chapter 5

TESTIMONY OF MICHAEL ROSE, VICE PRESIDENT, SUPPLY CHAIN VISIBILITY, JOHNSON AND JOHNSON HEALTH CARE SYSTEMS, INC. HEARING ON "SECURING OUR NATION'S PRESCRIPTION DRUG SUPPLY CHAIN"*

Thank you for your introduction, Mr. Chairman. I work for, and am representing, Johnson & Johnson Health Care Systems Inc. Johnson & Johnson Health Care Systems Inc. is the principal supply chain commercial entity within the Johnson & Johnson Family of Companies in the U.S. Thank you for the opportunity to speak here today. Securing Our Nation Supply Chain is an important concern for our company.

We believe it is vital that the patients who use our products receive our genuine products. We have already taken steps to secure our supply chain and protect our products. As a member of PhRMA (Pharmaceutical Research and Manufacturers of America) and BIO (Biotechnology Industry Organization), and a participant in PDSA - the Pharmaceutical Distribution Security Alliance, I will share with you our perspectives on serialization and track & trace, our serialization experience, and views on the proposed legislation.

---

* This is an edited, reformatted and augmented version of testimony presented April 25, 2013 before the House Committee on Energy and Commerce, Subcommittee on Health.

Serialization regulations have become increasingly common across many countries, including the European Union, Turkey, Argentina, China, India, and Brazil.

In the U.S., the California law requires manufacturers to serialize and pedigree all pharmaceutical products sold in the State of California — 50 percent of our products by January 1, 2015 and the remaining 50 percent by January 1, 2016. Additionally, more than 50 percent of the states have pedigree laws with varying approaches — that is, some require electronic pedigrees, others use paper, some start the pedigree with the primary distributor, others start it with the secondary wholesaler, etc.

This patchwork quilt of regulations leaves us with a complicated, inefficient regulatory landscape, creating unforeseen gaps where bad actors can introduce illicit drugs into the legitimate supply chain, thereby, placing our citizens at risk of counterfeit medicines. While the risk of encountering counterfeit medicines may be small within the legitimate domestic supply chain, when a patient receives a counterfeit medicine, the effects can be extremely dangerous, have long lasting impact, and can be even life threatening.

Our company believes that Federal serialization and track & trace legislation is necessary to properly secure our pharmaceutical supply chain by eliminating varying and conflicting state regulations. Federal legislation should help close the gaps where illicit drugs enter the U.S. supply chain, as well as provide additional mechanisms to help authenticate the legitimacy of medicines distributed and dispensed within the US to help protect the patients who use our medicines.

Next, I'd like to share our company's domestic serialization experience.

We are preparing our packaging sites, distribution centers, business and information technology systems to serialize and track & trace our products so that we can comply with the California e-Pedigree law. Here is an example of the first product that we have serialized for the U.S. market. This product is PREZISTA (darunavir) 600mg tablets.

For your reference, I have attached a label of serialized PREZISTA® 600mg to my testimony.

Let me draw your attention to the product license plate on the side of the label. This space is similar to the Prescription Drug Product Identifier prescribed in the House bill. We provide both machine and human readable forms for easy, accurate identification. Similarly, we apply a standard, serialized bar code to every homogeneous case to facilitate handling during distribution. This identification space complies with both the FDA's Serial

Number Identifier guidance, and the widely adopted international standards developed by GS1.

Additionally, we are establishing processes to exchange serialized data with the distributors who distribute our products, and with the pharmacies that dispense our medicines to patients who need them. We are required to provide this information to the distributors and pharmacies so that they can use it to help verify both the authenticity of the package as well as the transactions related to the product.

Bottom line, while it is complicated work and a lot still remains, we are doing our part to comply with the California law. However, if any other states were to adopt slightly different regulations, the inconsistencies could compromise the integrity of the supply chain, hence, supporting the need for Federal action now to secure our national supply chain.

Lastly, I would like to comment on the proposed legislation.

In 2011, our company, along with several other PhRMA and BIO members, and other supply chain participants helped form PDSA. PDSA's mission is to help enact a federal policy proposal for one unified national system enhancing the security of the domestic pharmaceutical distribution system for patients, and to define a migratory implementation pathway.

Johnson & Johnson Health Care Systems supports Representatives Latta and Matheson for tackling this important issue and making progress on a legislative solution. This legislation incorporates many of PDSA's proposed provisions including a uniform national standard with a phased implementation.

It is vitally important that both government and the private sector work together to protect our nation's drug supply in a manner that makes sense. We believe this legislation will help us secure the domestic pharmaceutical supply chain by providing additional protection to our citizens, patients who depend on the integrity of our medicines to treat their diseases and life-threatening conditions, from counterfeit medicines.

Johnson & Johnson Health Care Systems commitment to patient safety is unwavering. We look forward to Congress' enactment of this legislation, and we are committed to working with Congress, the FDA and our supply chain stakeholders to implement it successfully.

Again, thank you for the opportunity to provide this testimony to the Committee.

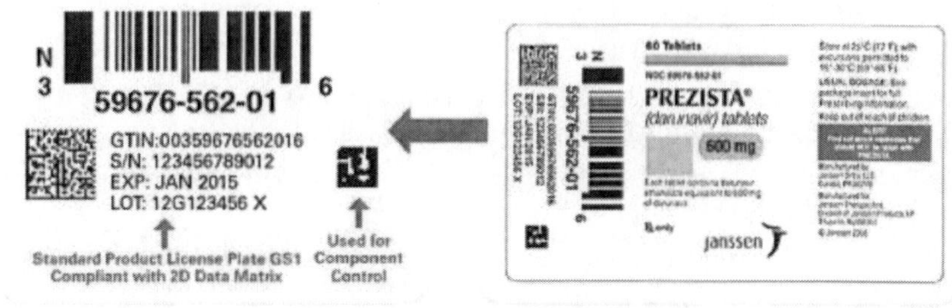

PREZISTA ® (darunavir) 600mg tablets

Exhibit 1. Serialized Label for PREZISTA® 600mg.

In: Securing the Pharmaceutical Supply Chain ISBN: 978-1-63463-448-9
Editor: Lenora White

Chapter 6

TESTIMONY OF TIM DAVIS, OWNER, BEAVER HEALTH MART PHARMACY. HEARING ON "SECURING OUR NATION'S PRESCRIPTION DRUG SUPPLY CHAIN"*

Chairman Pitts, Ranking Member Pallone and Members of the Committee:

Thank you for conducting this hearing and for providing me the opportunity to share my views and perspective as an independent pharmacist and small business owner on the issue of securing the pharmaceutical supply chain. My name is Tim Davis of Beaver, Pennsylvania. I am the owner of Beaver Health Mart Pharmacy and have been a practicing pharmacist for 12 years. I am here today representing the National Community Pharmacists Association (NCPA) which represents the pharmacist owners, managers and employees of more than 23,000 independent community pharmacies across the United States. These pharmacies provide about 40 percent of all community-based prescriptions.

It is my belief that the United States pharmaceutical supply chain is largely safe and secure. Most practicing pharmacists today have a heightened awareness of the possibility of counterfeit or diverted drugs and therefore recognize the critical importance of purchasing medications only from trusted trading partners or wholesalers.

* This is an edited, reformatted and augmented version of testimony presented April 25, 2013 before the House Committee on Energy and Commerce, Subcommittee on Health.

In addition, pharmacists, as an integral part of their training and day to day practice, are taught to carefully examine and make note of both the drug packaging and the appearance of the drug itself to be sure there are no suspicious anomalies.

It has been my observation that certain types of prescription medications tend to be the target of counterfeiters or "bad actors" in the supply chain. Relatively expensive drugs that can be easily produced and readily sold enable counterfeiters to create an attractive profit margin. Some drugs that I have seen that are particularly susceptible are lifestyle drugs, such as Viagra, as well as very costly injectable medications such as Procrit or more recently Avastin, that are not always carried in community pharmacies, but rather are dispensed through consolidated specialty pharmacies, health systems, or directly by physicians. In my career, I have seen one example of counterfeiting at a local level. We received manufacturer information that a particular drug, Procrit, had entered the drug supply chain in counterfeit form and we were instructed how to recognize the genuine product against the fake. Upon receipt of a daily shipment from our local wholesale distributor, we checked and found that an item that we received was indeed one of the counterfeit products. We immediately contacted and discussed the situation with our wholesaler. Our particular solution was actually to stop doing business with that wholesaler due to the lack of a believable and reliable response.

In response to concerns about the safety of prescription medications in the United States, over half of the states have passed "drug pedigree laws" that require drug products that move outside of "normal distribution" to be accompanied by a "pedigree" or record of prior transactions. However, this approach and the differences in each state's laws has created a "patchwork" of varying pedigree laws across the United States. Federal policy makers and supply chain participants alike have been discussing what a possible federal system to provide further assurances of supply chain security would look like for a number of years but due to the widely varying business models, financial resources and technological capabilities of those involved in the pharmaceutical supply chain, the process has not yielded a coherent, comprehensive national proposal yet on the federal level.

In the past, there have been numerous discussions about the practicality of a system that would track prescription drugs at the individual unit level. Pharmacists have had significant concerns about any system that would require each individual unit of medication to be electronically "scanned" upon arrival in a pharmacy due to the capital outlays that would be required and the time and labor costs associated with such a system. At the present time, the technologies that would be required to implement such a system are not fully developed and have not been designed or scaled to be feasible or affordable for use in individual community pharmacies.

Of great concern is the California "e-pedigree" law that will begin to be implemented for manufacturers in 2015 that will require the electronic tracking and tracing of all drug product packages, in real-time, in the drug distribution supply chain at the individual unit level through "electronic pedigrees" in an interoperable system. This well-intentioned system will require each individual participant in the supply chain to scan each individual item that will capture the transaction information. With each successive distribution, the e-pedigree must be updated with the new transaction data so that the e-pedigree continually grows as it makes its way to the pharmacy. In short, pharmacies will have the unenviable task of maintaining all drug pedigree data for all distributions above them and must be able to access it at any time. With the billions of drug product packages distributed, there will be billions of e-pedigrees and e-pedigree data that must be maintained and accessible—a massive amount of data. In addition, pharmacies must then pass back this information for each drug return.

The cost of compliance with this law will be extremely high especially for small community pharmacies—when factoring in both initial implementation and ongoing expenses necessary to maintain and access the data. Imposing these challenges particularly on small business supply chain participants like community pharmacies is not logical at a time when the nation is focused on trying to reduce the costs of healthcare.

All of these factors bring us to a place in which we need a uniform, federal framework to provide further assurances of supply chain security and that could be used to assist the FDA and other federal regulators in instances of recalls and other investigations. We need a reasonable, commonsense federal approach that will strike the appropriate balance between enhanced patient safety and minimizing unreasonable burdens on supply chain stakeholders, particularly small business pharmacies like myself.

NCPA is a member of the Pharmaceutical Distribution Security Alliance (PDSA), a working group comprised of representatives of all sectors of the pharmaceutical supply chain, which has been collaborating over the past year and a half to address supply chain security issues. The group has reached consensus around a number of different concepts. One of these concepts is that of establishing national requirements for wholesaler licensure standards. At the current time, there are some states in which the requirements necessary to obtain licensure as a drug wholesaler are less rigorous than others.

Raising the standards for wholesaler licensure in a uniform fashion would provide the community pharmacist at any location in the United States with an additional layer of confidence in the integrity of the medications purchased from such companies. The second concept is that of attaching a unique identifier to prescription drugs at the unit and case levels. Products would be identified at the unit and case level with a two dimensional matrix bar code including the serial number (SNI), lot number and expiration date for the product in machine and human readable form.

Once a product is serialized, this would essentially pave the way for all supply chain partners to eventually be able to use this data in increased ways and to be able to collaborate with one another to more easily locate particular products that may have been compromised in some way. The PDSA coalition has built consensus around being able to use the unique identifier information to track products at the lot-level. NCPA is pleased to note the inclusion of all of these consensus points in both the recently released House Discussion Draft and the Senate Discussion Draft. NCPA believes that the proposed lot-level system is one that could be built upon at some point in the future if it was determined that this was advisable and if there were significant inroads made on the associated technologies so that it would not be prohibitively expensive or burdensome for small business pharmacies.

I have a greater degree of confidence in the United States drug supply than I did just a few years ago—largely due to the heightened awareness of those in the supply chain to the possibility of counterfeit or diverted medications. That being said, community pharmacists take seriously our role in ensuring the safety of medications that we personally dispense to our patients and remain committed to working with our colleagues in the supply chain as well as with state and federal authorities to make any needed improvements. Moving forward, it is essential that all stakeholders make a concerted effort to keep the lines of communication open so that consumers can continue to trust the integrity of the medications that they depend on.

I appreciate the opportunity to address the Committee today and would be happy to address any questions that you may have.

Thank you

In: Securing the Pharmaceutical Supply Chain ISBN: 978-1-63463-448-9
Editor: Lenora White

Chapter 7

TESTIMONY OF ALLAN COUKELL, DIRECTOR, MEDICAL PROGRAMS, THE PEW CHARITABLE TRUSTS. HEARING ON "SECURING OUR NATION'S PRESCRIPTION DRUG SUPPLY CHAIN"*

Chairman Pitts, Ranking Member Pallone, and members of the Committee, thank you for the opportunity to provide testimony. My name is Allan Coukell. I direct drug and medical device work at The Pew Charitable Trusts.

Pew is an independent, nonpartisan research and public policy organization dedicated to serving the public.

Based on our analysis of the risks to the drug distribution system and the feasibility of addressing those risks, Pew supports the creation of a strong national system to protect American patients from the risks of counterfeit, stolen and diverted drugs.

The principles I will outline today are supported by other stakeholders, and I ask that a number of statements from consumer, patient, public health and industry groups be included in the record with my written testimony.[1]

There is general agreement on the need for a national system and how it would work. Manufacturers would put a unique serial number on each package of drug; the drugs would be tracked as they pass from hand to hand through

* This is an edited, reformatted and augmented version of testimony presented April 25, 2013 before the House Committee on Energy and Commerce, Subcommittee on Health.

the complex distribution system, and could be checked to ensure they are authentic.

This approach would bring us into line with standards in place in other countries and in individual U.S. states. Providing it creates a meaningful advance in safety, a single national system would be preferable to the current patchwork of 29 state drug pedigree laws.

Verification to Prevent Drug Diversion

A recent example demonstrates how verifying a serial number on a drug package could have prevented a significant crime and risk to patients.

In July 2012, the U.S. Attorney for the Southern District of New York charged 48 individuals in a large-scale criminal diversion scheme to buy prescription drugs "on the street" from patients, re-package them and re-sell them back into distribution through licensed pharmaceutical wholesalers, who in turn sold the drugs to pharmacies.[2] The scheme included medicines for HIV, schizophrenia, and asthma. In some cases, the criminals relabeled the drugs with new, fake labels.

This put patients at risk of counterfeit, outdated or mislabeled drugs. It also cost the Medicaid program in New York an estimated half-billion dollars. Similar schemes in other states are well documented, including one Tennessee in January of this year.[3]

This massive criminal recycling of government subsidized drugs could have been prevented by a serial number on a package. If the serial number was retired after the drugs reached the pharmacy, it would have been caught on its second trip around. Of course, that requires that the pharmacies and wholesalers purchasing the drug check that serial number. Without checking, the same serial number – real or fake – could be sold thousands of times over without detection.

Key Elements of a National System

Pharmaceutical manufacturers are already making investments in drug serialization technology. To justify the expense – and the preemption of strong state laws – it is essential that any federal law achieve the following within a reasonable time frame:

- Participation of all members of the supply chain
- Traceability of drugs at the package level (not merely by lot, which includes thousands or tens of thousands of bottles), and
- Routine checking of drug serial numbers.

We have identified widespread support for measures to ensure that all members of the supply chain participate in a national system. In a soon-to-be-released study that Pew conducted with the consulting firm Booz Allen Hamilton, ten manufacturers, ten wholesalers, and eleven pharmacies were asked what features of a national unit-level serialization and traceability system were important to them.[4] 80% of respondents said that all sectors in the supply chain needed to participate, without exception.

As I've mentioned, serialization beginning with the manufacturer and going through to verification by the dispenser is already in place or being implemented in other countries. China, Brazil, Turkey, Italy and the E.U. require (or will soon require) pharmacy authentication of serialized medicines in order to protect their citizens and prevent fraud.[5,6,7,8]

Fortunately, a number of technological advancements, including cloud-based solutions, such as the one used in a 2012 track and trace pilot involving Abbott, McKesson, and the U.S. Department of Veterans Affairs, demonstrate how pharmacies may authenticate drugs and participate in a traceability system through use of a simple web portal.[9,10]

Unit Level Serialization and Traceability

Another key to improved security of drug distribution is knowing who handles the drugs as they move from manufacturer, through a succession of wholesalers, to the pharmacy or hospital and, ultimately, to the patient.

A system that tracks drugs by the lot number instead of at the unit level may provide incremental benefit over the status quo, but would fail to catch unsafe drugs in many scenarios. A lot can contain numerous cases of many thousands of individual bottles. Each may be sold separately, and lot-level tracing does not allow industry or regulators to know who bought and sold a given drug during distribution.

Take the example of a product like growth hormone or some other performance enhancing drug, or of a drug in shortage, that investigators discover is being sold in the grey or black market. Without unit-level traceability, there is no way to know which pharmacy, hospital or clinic may have possessed the products or had the inventory "leak".

Today some companies are required to track a drug's transaction history through paper "pedigrees". An electronic system would be a welcome replacement to this paper-based paradigm; however, Congress should certainly not replace pedigrees, which are used by regulators and law enforcement, with a structure that does less to capture chain of custody than today's system.

ROUTINE CHECKING OF DRUG SERIAL NUMBERS

Regular checking of drug serial numbers by supply chain partners is a powerful way to ensure illegitimate products do not enter the distribution system and reach patients. In addition to preventing drug diversion, routing checking could also help the supply chain catch stolen and counterfeit drugs that criminals attempt to sell as legitimate products.

One example is the 2009 theft of a tractor-trailer containing 129,000 vials of insulin. This drug, which needs to be refrigerated, disappeared for a number of months before being sold back into distribution. Some of the stolen medicine was found at retail chain pharmacies in Texas, Georgia, and Kentucky, having passed through the hands of licensed wholesalers in at least two other states. But only 2 percent of that stolen inventory was ever recovered.[11,12]

In another case, thieves stole $75 million worth of pharmaceuticals from an Eli Lilly warehouse in Connecticut.[13] Early last year those stolen drugs were discovered stored in South Florida.[14] Had they been sold back into distribution no automated system would have flagged them for a pharmacy or wholesaler as stolen.

Counterfeits are another risk. Three times in a little more than a year, the FDA has announced the recovery of counterfeit Avastin® – a critical drug used to treat several types of cancer. In one of these cases, the supply chain included a licensed wholesaler in Tennessee. While we don't have full details about which members knew, or should have known, of the bogus product, the very existence of the fake drugs shows we can't be sanguine about the risks. Similarly, in 2001, counterfeit Serostim® — a human growth hormone used to treat AIDS-related wasting, was found in at least seven states and passed through multiple wholesalers.[15,16,17] EMD Serono, the manufacturer of Serostim,® has since put in place a secured distribution program with a unique serial number assigned to each vial that must be verified by the dispensing pharmacy.[18] Serono's program is an example of how drug distribution security can, and should, be improved.

CONCLUSION

I thank the Committee for holding this hearing and for its commitment to this issue. I also thank you for a discussion draft released this week. However this legislation, while it acknowledges the problem, does not offer a solution that will create meaningful protections for patients and does not address the comments that industry, patient, consumer, and public health groups made when Congress was contemplating this issue last year.

Congress first tried to address the kinds of risks I've been describing 25 years ago, through the Prescription Drug Marketing Act—a law that has never been fully implemented. Two years from now, California's comprehensive drug serialization law will begin to take effect. The opportunity today is great. We urge this committee to pursue a strong federal system that creates meaningful protections for patients.

Thank you again for the opportunity to testify, and I welcome your questions.

End Notes

[1] These groups include the American Society of Radiation Oncology; the Cancer Support Community; Children's Cause for Cancer Advocacy; Fight Colorectal Cancer; International Myeloma Foundation; Kidney Cancer Association; the Leukemia and Lymphoma Society; National Coalition for Cancer Survivorship; National Lung Cancer Partnership; Ovarian Cancer National Alliance; Pancreatic Cancer Action Network; Prevent Cancer Foundation; Sarcoma Foundation of America; Susan G. Komen for the Cure Advocacy Alliance; Us TOO International Prostate Cancer Education and Support Network; the American Public Health Association; the Association of State and Territorial Health Officials; the National Association of County and City Health Officials; the Trust for America's Health ; Center for Medical Consumers ; Community Catalyst; Consumers Union; National Consumers League; National Research Center for Women & Families; National Women's Health Network; U.S. PIRG; WoodyMatters, along with , EMD Serono and Hewlett Packard.

[2] United States Attorney's Office, Southern District of New York. Manhattan U.S. Attorney Announces Charges Against 48 Individuals in Massive Medicaid Fraud Scheme Involving the Diversion and Trafficking of Prescription Drugs. July 17, 2012. http://www.justice.gov/usao/nys/pressreleases/july12/prescriptiondrugs.html Accessed July 20, 2012.

[3] United States Attorney's Office for the Middle District of Tennessee. "Three Individuals Indicted For Prescription Drug Diversion Conspiracy". January 24, 2013. http://www.justice.gov/usao/tnm/pressReleases/2013/1-24- 13A.html

[4] Ten pharmaceutical manufacturers include five branded small molecule, one generic small molecule, three biopharmaceutical, and one contract packager. Ten pharmaceutical wholesalers include a range of business sizes, including one major national wholesaler. Eleven pharmaceutical dispensers include eight hospital pharmacies, one chain retail pharmacy, one independent pharmacy, and one mail-order pharmacy.

[5] Basta, Nicholas. "Serialization systems are going into operation around the world, but cross-industry collaboration awaits new legislation," Product Security Report, August 27, 2012 http://www.pharmaceuticalcommerce.com/index.php?pg=special report&articleid= 26610& keyword=2012%20pr oduct%20report-serialization-RxTEC.

[6] Turkish Ministry of Health. "G.D. of Pharmaceuticals and Pharmacies Guidance on Implementation of Identification and Barcoding of Medicinal Products for Human Use, Version 1.2" Ankara, 2009. http://www.clinicaltrial-storage.com/index.php/regulations-in-turkey-menu/89-turkish-drugs-barcode-guidancev1-2.

[7] Frost & Sullivan. "Mass Serialisation in the European Pharmaceutical Industry: Working Together on Mass Serialisation: Whose Responsibility is Ensuring Patient Safety?" 2008

[8] European Union. "Directive 2011/62/EU of the European Parliament and of the Council of 8." Official Journal of the European Union. June 2011. http://eur-lex.europa.eu/LexUriServ/LexUriServ.do?uri=OJ:L:2011:174:0074:0087:EN:PDF

[9] RxTrace. "The Significance of the Abbott, McKesson and VA Pilot". November 12, 2012 http://www.rxtrace.com/2012/11/the-significance-of-the-abbott-mckesson-and-va-pilot.html/

[10] Healthcare Distribution Management Association. "GHX Receives HDMA Distribution Management Award for 'First-of-its-Kind' Traceability Pilot". Press release. March 5, 2013 http://www.healthcaredistribution.org/pressroom/pr20130305dma.asp

[11] Ciolek, Michelle M., Special Agent, Office of Criminal Investigations, U.S. Food and Drug Administration. Affidavit in support of search warrant. July 21, 2009. USA v. Altec Medical Inc and RX healthcare Inc. Document number: 8:09-cr-00814-WMC.

[12] U.S. Food and Drug Administration. "Update to FDA Alert about Stolen insulin". August 26, 2009. http://www.fda.gov/ForConsumers/Consumerupdates/ucm180320.htm

[13] Forsaith, Chuck. Corporate Director, Supply Chain Security, Purdue Pharma L.P. "Cargo Theft." Presentation, 2010 PDA/FDA Pharmaceutical Supply Chain Workshop. Bethesda, MD. April 26-28, 2010.

[14] United States Attorney's Office, Southern District of Florida. Eleven Indicted in Pharmaceutical Thefts. May 3, 2012. http://www.justice.gov/usao/fls/PressReleases/120503-01.html. Accessed July 20, 2012.

[15] Serono, Inc. Serostim [somatropin (rDNA origin) for injection]. Press Release, January 2001 http://www.fda.gov/Safety/MedWatch/SafetyInformation/SafetyAlertsforHumanMedicalProducts/ucm173895.ht m. Accessed February 17, 2011.

[16] Otto, Alex. Counterfeit Serostim Found Nationwide. Pharmacy Today. American Pharmacists Association. March 1, 2001. http://www.medscape.com/viewarticle/406804. Accessed October 13, 2010.

[17] Dutchess Business Services Inc. v. Nevada State Board of Pharmacy. No. 46345. September 11, 2008 http://caselaw.findlaw.com/nv-supreme-court/1219556.html. Accessed February 17, 2011

[18] Williamson, Joyce P. Statement of Serono before the task force on drug importation. http://archive.hhs.gov/importtaskforce/session2/presentations/Serono.pdf Accessed February 17, 2011.

In: Securing the Pharmaceutical Supply Chain ISBN: 978-1-63463-448-9
Editor: Lenora White

Chapter 8

TESTIMONY OF CARMEN A. CATIZONE, EXECUTIVE DIRECTOR, NATIONAL ASSOCIATION OF BOARDS OF PHARMACY. HEARING ON "SECURING OUR NATION'S PRESCRIPTION DRUG SUPPLY CHAIN"*

Good morning Chairman Pitts, Ranking Member Pallone, and members of the Committee. The National Association of Boards of Pharmacy (NABP) appreciates the opportunity to appear before you today and provide information in regard to safeguarding the integrity of the nation's drug supply chain. I am Carmen Catizone, executive director of the Association.

NABP is the impartial professional organization that supports the state boards of pharmacy in protecting the public health. NABP aims to ensure the public's health and safety through its pharmacist license transfer, pharmacist competence assessment, and accreditation programs.

TWENTY FIVE YEARS OF "PROPOSED" AND" DELAYED"

The issues before the Committee are not new. In fact the timeline for trying to secure our nation's prescription drug supply chain extends farther

* This is an edited, reformatted and augmented version of testimony presented April 25, 2013 before the House Committee on Energy and Commerce, Subcommittee on Health.

back than many would care to admit and farther back than should be permitted. Quoting from the FDA's web site: "The Prescription Drug Marketing Act of 1987 (PDMA) was signed into law by the President April 12, 1988. The PDMA was enacted (1) to ensure that drug products purchased by consumers are safe and effective, and (2) to avoid the unacceptable risk to American consumers from counterfeit, adulterated, misbranded, subpotent, or expired drugs. The legislation was necessary to increase safeguards in the drug distribution system to prevent the introduction and retail sale of substandard, ineffective, or counterfeit drugs."

The activities that ensued since that time can best be described using two words, "proposed" and "delayed." The language found throughout multiple Federal Register notices since the implementation of the PDMA 25 years ago read similarly over and over. One example reads "On February 23, 2004 (69 FR 8105), FDA published a delay of the effective date of certain requirements in a final rule published in the Federal Register of December 3, 1999 (64 FR 67720)." The proposals presented by the FDA and supported by the states were continuously delayed and defeated by pressure from the industry.

NABP supports the implementation of a national system for the oversight and regulation of the prescription drug supply chain provided such system is comprehensive and does not discard the effective protections already in place and readied for implementation by the states, particularly California. In addition, NABP supports a national system provided it allows the states to have input into the development and recognizes the authority of the states to implement necessary modifications to address significant instances that may arise and were not contemplated or included in any national proposal. The national system supported by NABP is absolutely essential to the protection of the public we serve and to ensuring that the medications patients across the United States are dispensed or administered are safe and not counterfeit, diverted, or injurious in any way.

As some of you may be aware, NABP is intimately involved in the oversight of wholesale distributors as a result of our Verified-Accredited Wholesale Distributors (VAWD) program. To date, NABP has surveyed and accredited approximately 552 wholesale distributors across the states. As a result of those surveys and the valuable information and expertise that NABP gained, we can report to you that some of the issues originally driving the enactment of the PDMA in 1987 have been addressed and resolved. There are, however, still a number of critical concerns that threaten the distribution supply chain that must be addressed. It was our hope that many if not all of these issues would be the focus of legislation proposed and adopted by the

House and Senate. Our analysis of the legislative proposal released just a few days ago indicates that it may not address these serious issues.

Besides some of the high profile abuses that have been reported in the media, NABP observed first hand and reported to the applicable state and federal authorities breaches in, and compromises to, the prescription drug supply chain. These breaches and compromises include, but are not limited to, the lack of complete or the absence entirely of pedigrees or other required transaction documents, pedigrees or other transaction documents that indicate a product passed through multiple entities some licensed and others not, multiple wholesaler companies located in a one-room strip mall business office claiming some form of common ownership, wholesalers receiving and storing products under conditions that render the medications adulterated or contaminated, and wholesalers and pharmacies, establishing as their sole operating model the purchase and sale of shortage drugs and inflating the prices of these products by a thousand-fold – an unconscionable action when it comes to drugs that are needed by patients suffering from life-threatening conditions such as cancer.

THE STATES SERVE AS THE LAST DEFENSE FOR PATIENTS AND CONSUMERS

The states are both the front line and last line of defense in the prescription drug supply chain. Since the inception of the PDMA, the states have had to forge a system of oversight and regulation to protect the integrity of products in the supply chain absent a national system because for 25 years the industry has fought such state and federal efforts and delayed implementation of a proposed solution.

The Institute of Medicine's report, "Countering the Problem of Falsified and Substandard Drugs," notes that "crime and corruption drive the business of falsified medicines." The report further documents that "medicines can change hands many times in myriad countries before they reach patients." One of the primary recommendations of the IOM report is critical to the considerations before this Committee and bears noting this morning:

> "The IOM committee calls for strengthening the drug distribution system in order to improve the quality of medicine and protect consumers. Top among its priorities is restricting the U.S. wholesale market to firms vetted by the National Association of Boards of

Pharmacy. This action would tighten the American drug distribution chain and build momentum for better controls on drug wholesalers in developing countries."

RECOMMENDATIONS

1) Support the existing and successful public-private partnership system, VAWD that NABP established with the states and is endorsed by the Institute of Medicine. NABP asks the Committee to consider the priority recommendation of the IOM and support the effective public private partnership that currently exists between NABP and state and federal regulators, protecting the integrity of the drug supply chain at no cost to the American taxpayers.
2) No further delays. NABP believes that the time has long passed for any continued delay in addressing and resolving the challenges confronting our nation's prescription drug supply chain. The timeline for federal action in the proposed legislation extends the wait of consumers and patients for a protected supply chain to 35 years! California's requirements can be operational over the next three years and help to build the uniform and national standards that all stakeholders support. In comparison over the past 30 years the following notable advances occurred:

a) Internet, broadband, www (browser and html)
b) PC/laptop computers
c) Mobile phones
d) E-mail
e) DNA testing and sequencing/human genome mapping
f) Magnetic Resonance Imaging (MRI)
g) Microprocessors
h) Fiber optics
i) Office software (spreadsheets, word processors)
j) Non-invasive laser/robotic surgery (laparoscopy)
k) Open-source software and services (e.g., Linux, Wikipedia)
l) Light-emitting diodes
m) Liquid crystal display (LCD)
n) GPS systems
o) Online shopping/e-commerce/auctions (e.g., eBay)

p) Media file compression (jpeg, mpeg, mp3)
q) Microfinance
r) Photovoltaic solar energy
s) Large- scale wind turbines
t) Social networking via the Internet
u) Graphic user interface (GUI)
v) Digital photography/videography
w) RFID and applications (e.g., EZ Pass)
x) Genetically modified plants
y) Bio fuels
z) Bar codes and scanners
   - ATMs
   - Stents
   - SRAM flash memory
   - Anti-retroviral treatment for AIDS

3) All participants in the supply chain must be accountable. Exemptions should not be granted to pharmacies.
4) The tracking and traceability of products should be to the package level and operational in 2015 and 2016 in order not to retreat on the advances made by California and the timelines already committed to by a growing number of the industry.
5) Pharmacies and wholesale distributors must append and pass pedigrees or other equivalent transaction documents within the next two to four years.
6) Establish a process for the routine and regular verification of product serial numbers.
7) Provide the Food and Drug Administration (FDA) with the full scope of authority and resources needed to implement and enforce a national system.

CONCLUSION

NABP thanks the Committee for the opportunity to appear today and present information and concerns from the state boards of pharmacy. The Association and its member state agencies support a comprehensive national solution to the challenges facing the integrity of our prescription drug supply chain. However, that supply chain must place public safety first and not undo the significant advances made by the states and FDA to ensure that American citizens across the country receive safe and effective medications.

Thank you.

In: Securing the Pharmaceutical Supply Chain ISBN: 978-1-63463-448-9
Editor: Lenora White

Chapter 9

Statement of Deborah M. Autor, Deputy Commissioner for Global Regulatory Operations and Policy, FDA. Hearing on "Securing The Pharmaceutical Supply Chain"*

Introduction

Good morning, Chairman Harkin and Members of the Committee. I am Deborah Autor, Deputy Commissioner for Global Regulatory Operations and Policy at the Food and Drug Administration (FDA or the Agency) in the Department of Health and Human Services (HHS). Thank you for the opportunity to discuss the safety of the American drug supply.

When President Franklin Delano Roosevelt established the modern FDA in 1938, the percentage of medical products imported into the United States was minimal. Today the landscape is reversed. Nearly 40 percent of the drugs Americans take are made elsewhere, and about 80 percent of active pharmaceutical ingredients (APIs) used in drugs manufactured in the United States come from outside our borders—from more than 150 countries, many with less sophisticated manufacturing and regulatory systems than our own. In addition to the sheer volume of imports and foreign facilities, there has been an increase in the variety of sources, shippers, methods of transportation and

* This is an edited, reformatted and augmented version of a statement presented September 14, 2011 before the Senate Committee on Health, Education, Labor and Pensions.

supply chain complexity of imported products, and our current authorities have not kept pace with the challenges of the current global marketplace. Combined, these factors create great challenges to FDA and industry in ensuring that all drugs are high quality and travel safely throughout their complex supply chains. These factors also provide opportunities for criminals to adulterate drugs for economic or other malevolent reasons.

When we refer to the drug supply chain, we are talking about the increasingly complex path that medical products travel, from raw source materials to finished products for consumers. At every stage in this process, opportunities arise for the product to be contaminated, diverted, counterfeited, or otherwise adulterated. The Internet presents an additional layer of complexity by introducing more players into the system and more opportunities for criminals to reach consumers. Our efforts to secure the supply chain both in the United States and abroad include minimizing risks that arise anywhere along the supply chain continuum, from sourcing a product's raw material, ingredients, and components through the product's manufacture, storage, transit, sale and distribution. A breach at any point in this continuum could lead to dangerous and even deadly outcomes for consumers. Supply chain safety threats also impact manufacturers' bottom lines due to costs associated with both recalls and decreased public confidence.

As Members of this Committee well know, this threat is not purely hypothetical. Recent incidents of adulteration, counterfeiting, and cargo theft have posed serious threats to public health. The consequences, throughout the world, have been tragic. In recent years, glycerin in fever medicine, cough syrup, and teething products was adulterated with the highly toxic solvent, diethylene glycol (DEG), resulting in the deaths of adults and children in Panama, and children in Haiti and Nigeria. Over the last 20 years, drug products containing glycerin contaminated with DEG have caused an estimated 570 deaths worldwide. Also in 2007, pet food adulterated with the industrial chemical melamine and cyanuric acid sickened several thousand pets in our country. The same contaminant was added to infant formula in China, fatally poisoning six babies and making 300,000 others gravely ill. And Members of this Committee are well aware of the 2008 heparin contamination crisis that resulted in several deaths and cases of serious illness.

Counterfeit drugs raise significant public health concerns, because their safety and effectiveness is unknown. A counterfeited drug could be made up of a substance that is toxic to patients. But even a non-toxic counterfeit drug with a substitute or no active ingredient could prove harmful to patients who take it, thinking that they are taking a lifesaving or life-sustaining medication.

In 2003, over $20 million in illegally imported and counterfeit Lipitor, a popular cholesterol-lowering drug, was distributed throughout the United States. The source and manufacturing methods of the product were unknown and had the potential to endanger patients.

Cargo thefts of prescription drugs also pose a significant public health risk. In 2009 alone, an estimated 46 drug cargo thefts occurred, valued at a total of $184 million. These incidents are concerning to companies and consumers alike. Cargo thefts can cost drug manufacturers millions of dollars. They can also put consumers at risk because the stolen drugs may not have been stored or handled properly or may have been tampered with while outside of the legitimate supply chain. In March of 2010, thieves broke into a warehouse and stole $75 million worth of prescription drug products, including chemotherapy, antidepressants, and blood-thinners. These products have not yet been recovered, and we fear they could be distributed, in spite of public warning. In 2009, stolen insulin was reintroduced into the drug supply and caused adverse events in patients. The stolen insulin, which requires refrigeration, lost its potency and did not provide the needed glucose control.

In our increasingly complex and globalized world, additional authorities could be important tools to help support FDA's efforts to protect the safety of imports and the health of our citizens. New regulatory authorities may also help ensure that industry takes principal responsibility for the security and integrity of their supply chains and the quality control systems they use to produce medical products for the American people. FDA's efforts are also critical to ensuring product integrity. As such, we intend to further transform FDA over the next decade from a predominantly domestically focused Agency, operating in a globalized world, to an Agency fully prepared for a regulatory environment in which product safety and quality know no borders.

In June, FDA published a special report, "Pathway to Global Product Safety and Quality," our global strategy and action plan that will allow us to more effectively oversee the quality, safety, and efficacy of all products that reach U.S. consumers in the future. The Agency is developing a new, more global operating model that relies on strengthened collaboration, improved information sharing and gathering, data-driven risk analytics, and the smart allocation of resources, leveraging the combined efforts of government, industry, and public- and private-sector third parties. Toward this goal, FDA Commissioner Margaret Hamburg created a directorate focused on grappling with the truly global nature of today's world—food and medical product production and supply, as well as the science that undergirds the products we regulate— so that FDA can move from being a regulator of domestic products to one overseeing worldwide enterprises. She appointed me as Deputy Commissioner for Global Regulatory Operations and Policy to provide broad direction and support to FDA's Office of Regulatory Affairs and Office of International Programs, with a responsibility to address the challenges of globalization and import safety a top priority in the years to come and to ensure that we fully integrate our domestic and international programs to best promote and protect the health of the public. I appreciate the opportunity to testify before you in my new role and look forward to working together to address the challenges we face in protecting our nation's health in this increasingly globalized world.

Steps to Secure Our Nation's Drug Supply Chain

FDA has undertaken a wide range of activities aimed at addressing the challenges and opportunities of globalization, including efforts to harmonize scientifically rigorous standards internationally, to share scientific and technical expertise with our fellow regulators, to provide training around the world in crucial regulatory disciplines, to strengthen detection, surveillance and assessment systems, and to design innovative risk-modeling systems.

We now have permanent FDA overseas posts in Beijing, Shanghai, and Guangzhou, China; New Delhi and Mumbai, India; San Jose, Costa Rica; Mexico City, Mexico; Santiago, Chile; Brussels, Belgium; London, England; and Parma, Italy. This year, we have opened posts in Amman, Jordan and Pretoria, South Africa. These offices enable us to have a regional presence around the world and serve as important hubs for improved coordination with regulatory authorities and industry in other nations. They also conduct and facilitate inspections and other on-the-ground activities in foreign sites. We have more than 30 agreements with foreign counterpart agencies to share inspection reports and other non-public information that can help us make better decisions about the quality and safety of foreign products.

When governments collaborate to strengthen safety standards, the results are safer, higher-quality products and enhanced economic development through a productive industry and a strong, reliable export market. The arrangement is mutually beneficial. To a large extent, our success or failure in this effort will be contingent on the relationships we establish with our foreign partners. That is why we are working closely with our sister regulatory authorities, international and national organizations, and industry to leverage resources to accomplish FDA's mission. Especially in the area of good manufacturing practices for drugs, we already have agreed with major foreign counterparts on some harmonized international standards. By using the results of their inspections to assure us that their manufacturing plants are adhering to our agreed standard, we free up our inspectional resources to help ensure that such manufacturing practices are being followed in other, higher-risk parts of the world. This also lessens the regulatory burden on industry, by allowing companies to manufacture to a common standard and to undergo fewer inspections by multiple authorities.

After Heparin

The 2008 heparin contamination crisis is a case study in the vulnerabilities of the global supply chain. Heparin is a widely used injectable anticoagulant, derived from the mucosal tissue of pigs. In early 2008, contaminated heparin from China was associated with an increase in deaths in the United States. Whatever was contaminating this imported heparin could not be identified by the tests used at the time. After launching a far-ranging investigation, FDA scientists, working closely with academia and industry, developed a test methodology that identified a previously unknown contaminant in Chinese-manufactured heparin. The contaminated heparin contained oversulfated chondroitin sulfate (OSCS), an intentionally added adulterant. An outbreak of blue ear pig disease had killed off a large portion of China's pig population, creating an incentive for criminals to seek an alternative that mimicked the chemical makeup of heparin but, tragically, proved dangerous to consumers.

FDA publicly referred to the heparin contamination crisis as a "wake-up call." It was an alert not only for FDA, but also for U.S. citizens, industry, and lawmakers about our dependence on a globalized drug supply and the key vulnerabilities in our drug supply chain. FDA has taken a number of significant steps to safeguard the U.S. supply of this medically necessary drug. The Agency invested considerable resources to inspect heparin manufacturing and testing facilities related to the supply of heparin in the United States. Additionally, the United States Pharmacopoeia, a standards-setting organization upon which FDA relies, now calls for the testing of heparin to detect the presence of OSCS, the contaminant that sickened patients in 2008. FDA has also implemented heparin-specific import surveillance including an import alert and multiple warning letters to ensure that adulterated heparin does not enter our borders.

But our efforts have not stopped there. The heparin crisis was a crime of opportunity, and we need to minimize these opportunities. We are committed to putting preventive measures in place that will protect American consumers from adulteration of all imported drugs. We combine risk-based approaches with sound scientific evidence to protect the public from adulterated and unsafe drugs. The Agency takes several factors into account in determining whether a particular drug ingredient may be at risk for adulteration. For example, when a drug ingredient depends on raw materials that are particularly expensive, criminals may have extra incentive to find a cheaper alternative to the expensive ingredient. If the cheaper alternative can mimic the chemical activity of the product and thereby go undetected by standard testing, as was the case in the heparin and melamine incidents, the risk of adulteration is higher. To date, FDA has systematically ranked more than 1,000 APIs in order of their respective risk of adulteration, based on a multi-factorial, risk-based model we developed. A subset of these higher-risk ingredients is targeted for additional sampling and special testing at the border. In addition, FDA is working to reduce the risk that counterfeit or adulterated drug products reach consumers in the U.S. market by developing standards for a track-and-trace system that would enable the identification of these products and facilitate efforts to recall them.

Through the creation of my position and other activities at the Agency, we have made addressing the challenges of globalization a top priority. To support this effort, FDA can benefit from new legislative authorities that are, at a minimum, commensurate with those of its major global counterparts.

Drug Safety Authorities

In general, new regulatory authorities may help ensure that industry takes principal responsibility for the security and integrity of its supply chains and the quality control systems it uses to produce drugs for the American people. In an era of globalization, new authorities can help to level the playing field between domestic and foreign manufacturers, ensure product safety and provide FDA with the information it needs to protect consumers. Those authorities may include:

Leveling the Playing Field

- Refusal of product admission to the United States if inspection of the manufacturing facility is delayed, limited, or denied – this authority is critical to providing a strong incentive for foreign facilities to allow FDA to perform inspections and to permit FDA to exclude from domestic commerce products whose foreign manufacturers or facilities try to avoid subjecting themselves to the same requirements as domestic manufacturers and facilities. This authority is not currently explicit in FDA's law for any product other than foods.

- Require information upon importation – the Agency can refuse entry of an import that appears from examination of samples or otherwise to be adulterated or misbranded, but FDA lacks authority to require certification or other assurance of compliance with applicable standards or requirements as a condition of importation, consistent with FDA's standards and requirements for the domestic drug supply. This is the opposite of the approach taken by many other countries, which place the burden on the importer or product owner to prove that its drug is compliant with country requirements.
- Quality management systems – FDA currently works with industry to ensure that individual companies have effective quality management systems in place; however, additional statutory authority could place greater responsibility on manufacturers to account for the quality and provenance of the materials that go into their products. This would level the playing field between the companies that work diligently on their quality management systems to provide high quality products, and those that do not.
- While FDA does not seek to interfere with regulatory authorities outside the United States, having express authority to address threats to U.S. consumers, whenever and wherever they may arise, is critical.

Increasing Drug Safety

- Mandatory recall authority – while in most instances firms eventually agree to voluntarily recall drugs that FDA believes pose a risk, FDA lacks the authority to compel such recalls and critical time can be lost in negotiations between FDA and a firm, leaving the public exposed to potentially serious health risks. The Agency currently has mandatory recall authority for medical devices, infant formula, and now many other foods, but not for drugs.
- Administrative destruction at the border – absent this streamlined authority, FDA is often forced to return violative products to their senders because the current process for destruction requires a hearing, which is time-consuming and costly. Foreign drugs can then find their

way back to U.S. ports of entry several times, posing a potential threat to consumers and wasting critical resources that could be better spent identifying new threats. This authority would level the playing field for those who produce compliant products, whether located in the United States or abroad.

- Administrative detention – while FDA has the authority to administratively detain illegal foods and medical devices in U.S. commerce, it does not have a similar authority for drugs. Currently, we cannot immediately detain dangerous drug products when we find them. Absent this immediate tool, consumers can be exposed to unnecessary risks.
- Enhanced criminal and civil penalties for foreign and domestic suppliers – statutory changes could help to deter would-be criminals from targeting drug products, and bring FDA's penalties in line with those for other serious federal health and safety violations.

Increasing Information

- Modernization of drug registration and listing – revising these statutory provisions may improve the timeliness, completeness, and accuracy of FDA's current registration and listing information, making sure FDA has accurate and up-to-date information about foreign and domestic parties involved in medical product manufacture.
- Notification to FDA – this authority would permit FDA to require foreign and domestic companies to provide complete information on threats such as counterfeiting, theft, noncompliance with regulatory standards, mislabeling or misbranding, or other threats to the security of the drug supply chain. Among other things, this would allow FDA to better spot emerging risks and trends across companies and then inform industry or take other proactive, preventive steps.
- Unique facility identifier – the absence of a system of unique drug facility identifiers, such as a D-U-N-S number, submitted to FDA both as a condition of registration and import, makes it difficult for FDA to properly follow threats up the supply chain and makes it more difficult to get different systems, including at different agencies, to properly cross-reference.
- Authority to share certain non-public information with other regulatory agencies and foreign governments – this authority would

allow FDA to share certain information that could lead to timely identification, prevention, and resolution of emerging threats. Our ability to form global coalitions of regulators will be hampered if we cannot share critical information with our trusted partners.

- Track and trace – requiring a cost-effective track-and-trace system for all drug products throughout the supply chain would improve the security and integrity of the drug supply and ensure transparency and accountability of product manufacturing and distribution, whether the product is manufactured domestically or internationally.
- In our increasingly complex and globalized world, these additional authorities represent important tools to help support efforts to protect the safety of imports and the health of our citizens.

CONCLUSION

Given the challenges and threats posed by an increasingly globalized marketplace, we must modernize our approach to drug safety. We appreciate the comments of Chairman Harkin and Ranking Member Enzi in July in support of including legislation in the reauthorization of the Prescription Drug User Fee Act (PDUFA) to address the challenges of globalization. We look forward to continuing to work together to achieve our shared goal of protecting American consumers. I would be happy to answer any questions.

In: Securing the Pharmaceutical Supply Chain
Editor: Lenora White
ISBN: 978-1-63463-448-9

Chapter 10

DRUG SAFETY: FDA FACES CHALLENGES OVERSEEING THE FOREIGN DRUG MANUFACTURING SUPPLY CHAIN. STATEMENT OF MARCIA CROSSE, DIRECTOR, HEALTH CARE, U.S. GOVERNMENT ACCOUNTABILITY OFFICE. HEARING ON "SECURING THE PHARMACEUTICAL SUPPLY CHAIN"*

WHY GAO DID THIS STUDY

Globalization has placed increasing demands on the Food and Drug Administration (FDA) in ensuring the safety and effectiveness of drugs marketed in the United States. The pharmaceutical industry has increasingly relied on global supply chains in which each manufacturing step may be outsourced to foreign establishments. As part of its efforts, FDA may conduct inspections of foreign drug manufacturing establishments, but there are concerns that the complexity of the drug manufacturing supply chain and the volume of imported drugs has created regulatory challenges for FDA. FDA

* This is an edited, reformatted and augmented version of a statement presented September 14, 2011 before the Senate Committee on Health, Education, Labor and Pensions.

has begun taking steps to address some of these concerns, such as the establishment of overseas offices.

This statement discusses (1) FDA's inspection of foreign drug manufacturing establishments, (2) the information FDA has on these establishments, and (3) recent FDA initiatives to improve its oversight of the supply chain. The statement presents findings based primarily on GAO reports since 2008 related to FDA's oversight of the supply chain. These reports include *Food and Drug Administration: Overseas Offices Have Taken Steps to Help Ensure Import Safety, but More Long-Term Planning Is Needed* (GAO-10-960, Sept. 30, 2010) and *Drug Safety: FDA Has Conducted More Foreign Inspections and Begun to Improve Its Information on Foreign Establishments, but More Progress Is Needed* (GAO-10-961, Sept. 30, 2010). GAO supplemented this prior work with updated information obtained from FDA in August and September 2011.

What GAO Found

Inspections of foreign drug manufacturers are an important element of FDA's oversight of the supply chain, but GAO's prior work showed that FDA conducts relatively few such inspections. In 2008, GAO reported that in fiscal year 2007 FDA inspected 8 percent of foreign establishments subject to inspection and estimated that, at that rate, it would take FDA about 13 years to inspect all such establishments. GAO recommended that FDA increase the number of foreign inspections it conducts at a frequency comparable to domestic establishments with similar characteristics. FDA subsequently increased the number of foreign establishment inspections. FDA's inspection efforts in fiscal year 2009 represent a 27 percent increase in the number of inspections it conducted, when compared to fiscal year 2007—424 and 333 inspections, respectively. However, FDA officials acknowledged that FDA is far from achieving foreign drug inspection rates comparable to domestic inspection rates—the agency inspected 1,015 domestic establishments in fiscal year 2009. Also, the types of inspections FDA conducts generally do not include all parts of the drug supply chain. Conducting inspections abroad also continues to pose unique challenges for the agency. For example, FDA faces limits on its ability to require foreign establishments to allow it to inspect their facilities. Furthermore, logistical issues preclude FDA from conducting unannounced inspections, as it does for domestic establishments.

GAO previously reported that FDA lacked complete and accurate information on foreign drug manufacturing establishments—information critical to understanding the supply chain. In 2008, GAO reported that FDA databases contained incorrect information about foreign establishments and did not contain an accurate count of foreign establishments manufacturing drugs for the U.S. market. FDA's lack of information hampers its ability to inspect foreign establishments. GAO recommended that FDA address these deficiencies. FDA has taken steps to do so, but has not yet fully addressed GAO's concerns.

Given the difficulties that FDA has faced in inspecting and obtaining information on foreign drug manufacturers, and recognizing that more inspections alone are not sufficient to meet the challenges posed by globalization, the agency has begun to implement other initiatives to improve its oversight of the drug supply chain. FDA's overseas offices have engaged in a variety of activities to help ensure the safety of imported products, such as training foreign stakeholders to help enhance their understanding of FDA regulations. GAO recommended that FDA enhance its strategic and workforce planning, which FDA agreed it would do. FDA has also taken other positive steps, such as developing initiatives that would assist its oversight of products at the border, although these are not yet fully implemented. Finally, FDA officials identified statutory changes that FDA believes it needs to help improve its oversight of drugs manufactured in foreign establishments. For example, in place of the current requirement that FDA inspect domestic establishments every 2 years, officials indicated the agency would benefit from a risk-based inspection process with flexibility to determine the frequency with which both foreign and domestic establishments are inspected. In light of the growing dependence upon drugs manufactured abroad and the potential for harm, FDA needs to act quickly to implement changes across a range of activities in order to better assure the safety and availability of drugs for the U.S. market.

* * *

Chairman Harkin,
Ranking Member Enzi, and Members of the Committee:

I am pleased to be here today to discuss the Food and Drug Administration's (FDA) oversight of the nation's drug supply chain.[1] Globalization has placed increasing demands on FDA, which is responsible for the oversight of drugs marketed in the United States, regardless of whether they are manufactured in foreign or domestic establishments.[2] While Americans once used drugs that were mostly manufactured domestically, this is no longer the case. According to FDA, the number of drug products manufactured at foreign establishments has more than doubled since 2002, with China and India accounting for the greatest shares of this growth. In addition, the pharmaceutical industry has increasingly relied on global supply chains in which each manufacturing step may be outsourced to foreign establishments. The complexity of the drug supply chain, the volume of imported drugs, and the number of foreign establishments producing these drugs have created regulatory challenges for FDA. The danger associated with an insecure supply chain was highlighted in January 2008, when FDA responded to a crisis involving the contamination of the active pharmaceutical ingredient (API) used to manufacture heparin,[3] a medication used to prevent and treat blood clots. The contaminated heparin, which was associated with numerous adverse events—including deaths—came from a facility in China. During its investigation, FDA determined that some manufacturers were not adequately safeguarding their heparin supply chains.[4]

In recent years we have reported on several aspects of FDA's ability to protect Americans from unsafe and ineffective drugs entering our supply chain.[5] Amidst growing concerns with the increasing demands placed on the agency, including its ability to ensure the quality of drugs manufactured overseas, we added FDA's oversight of medical products to our High-Risk Series.[6] FDA has acknowledged that globalization has fundamentally changed the environment for regulating pharmaceutical products and the agency has begun taking steps to address some of these concerns, such as the establishment of overseas offices.[7]

My remarks today will focus primarily on information collected for several reports we issued since 2008 that specifically cite concerns we identified related to FDA's oversight of the manufacturing side of the supply chain for drugs produced by overseas establishments for marketing in the United States.[8] Specifically, I will discuss (1) FDA's inspections of foreign drug manufacturing establishments, which are intended to assure that the safety and quality of drugs are not jeopardized by poor manufacturing practices; (2) the information FDA has on these establishments; and (3) recent FDA initiatives to improve its oversight of the supply chain.

For our work reviewing FDA's inspections of foreign drug manufacturing establishments, we obtained and analyzed FDA data on foreign and domestic drug manufacturing establishment inspections conducted from fiscal years

2007 to 2009. We also examined methods used by FDA to select establishments for inspection. For our work examining how FDA responded to the heparin crisis, we reviewed actions FDA took during the crisis period, which FDA defined as January 2008 through May 2008. We also interviewed FDA officials and drug manufacturers and reviewed FDA documents, such as inspection reports and internally produced summaries (e.g., a time line of events related to the crisis).

For our work reviewing the information FDA has on foreign drug manufacturing establishments, we obtained data from FDA's registration database on the number of establishments registered to market their drugs in the United States.[9] We also obtained data from FDA's import database on the number of establishments that have manufactured drugs that were shipped to the United States.[10] We reviewed FDA's initiatives for improving the accuracy of the agency's data on foreign establishments contained in these databases, which are both used to manage the foreign drug inspection program.

For our work reviewing recent FDA initiatives intended to improve the agency's oversight of foreign drug manufacturing establishments, we reviewed documentation and interviewed FDA officials from each of FDA's five overseas offices to learn about their activities, challenges, accomplishments, and strategic and workforce planning. For three of the overseas offices—China, India, and Latin America—we interviewed office staff and others, such as officials from FDA's foreign regulatory counterparts, during on-site visits in February and March 2010. We also reviewed documents related to the agency's efforts to augment its existing information on foreign drug establishments, such as information obtained from foreign regulatory authorities. We supplemented that prior work with updated information that we received from FDA in August and September 2011.

We conducted the work for the performance audits on which this statement is based from September 2007 to September 2008, June 2009 to September 2010, and from August to September 2011 for selected updates. Our work was conducted in accordance with generally accepted government auditing standards. Those standards require that we plan and perform the audit to obtain sufficient, appropriate evidence to provide a reasonable basis for our findings and conclusions based on our audit objectives. We believe that the evidence obtained provides a reasonable basis for our findings and conclusions based on our audit objectives.

Background

As part of its efforts to ensure the safety and quality of imported drugs, FDA may conduct inspections of foreign establishments manufacturing drugs, including APIs, that are imported into the United States. FDA relies on these establishment inspections to determine compliance with current good manufacturing practice regulations (GMP).[11] The purpose of these inspections is to ensure that foreign establishments meet the same requirements as domestic establishments to ensure the quality, purity, potency, safety, and efficacy of drugs marketed in the United States.

Requirements governing FDA's inspection of foreign and domestic establishments differ. Specifically, FDA is required to inspect every 2 years those domestic establishments that manufacture drugs in the United States, but there is no comparable requirement for inspecting foreign establishments that market their drugs in the United States.[12] However, drugs manufactured by foreign establishments that are offered for import may be refused entry to the United States if FDA determines— through the inspection of an establishment, a physical examination of drugs when they are offered for import at a point of entry, or otherwise— that there is sufficient evidence of a violation of applicable laws or regulations.[13]

FDA conducts two primary types of drug manufacturing establishment inspections. Preapproval inspections of domestic and foreign establishments may be conducted before FDA will approve a new drug to be marketed in the United States. In addition, FDA conducts GMP inspections at establishments manufacturing drugs already marketed in the United States to determine ongoing compliance with laws and regulations.

FDA Conducts Relatively Few Inspections of Foreign Drug Establishments

Although inspections of foreign drug manufacturing establishments—which are intended to assure that the safety and quality of drugs are not jeopardized by poor manufacturing practices—are an important element of FDA's oversight of the supply chain, our previous work has shown that FDA conducts relatively few inspections of the establishments that it considers subject to inspection. Specifically, in our 2008 report, we estimated that FDA inspected 8 percent of such foreign drug establishments in fiscal year 2007. At this rate, we estimated that it would take FDA about 13 years to inspect all foreign establishments the agency considers subject to inspection. In 2010, we reported that FDA had increased its inspection efforts in fiscal year 2009. We estimated that FDA inspected 11 percent of foreign establishments subject to inspection and it would take FDA about 9 years to inspect all such establishments at this rate. FDA's inspection efforts in fiscal year 2009 represent a 27 percent increase in the number of inspections the agency conducted when compared to fiscal year 2007—424 and 333 inspections, respectively.[14] In contrast, FDA conducts more inspections of domestic establishments and the agency inspects these establishments more frequently. For example, in fiscal year 2009, FDA conducted 1,015 domestic inspections, inspecting approximately 40 percent of domestic establishments. We estimated that at this rate FDA inspects domestic establishments approximately once every 2.5 years. To address these discrepancies, we recommended that FDA conduct more inspections to ensure that foreign establishments manufacturing drugs currently marketed in the United States are inspected at a frequency comparable to domestic establishments with similar characteristics.[15] FDA agreed that the agency should be conducting more foreign inspections, but FDA officials have since acknowledged that the agency is far from achieving foreign drug inspection rates comparable to domestic inspection rates and, without significant increases to its inspectional capacity, the agency's ability to close this gap is highly unlikely.[16]

In addition to conducting few foreign drug manufacturing inspections, the types of inspections FDA conducts generally do not include all parts of the drug supply chain. For example, FDA officials told us during our review of the contaminated heparin crisis that the agency typically does not inspect manufacturers of source material[17]—which are not required to be listed on applications to market drugs in the United States—and generally limits its inspections to manufacturers of the finished product and APIs. Furthermore, once FDA conducts an inspection of a foreign drug manufacturer, it is unlikely that the agency will inspect it again, as the majority of the foreign inspections FDA conducts are to inform decisions about the approval of new drugs before they are marketed for sale in the United States.

Despite increases in foreign drug establishment inspections in recent years, FDA continues to face unique challenges conducting inspections abroad. Specifically, as we identified in our 2008 report on FDA's foreign drug inspections, FDA continues to experience challenges related to limits on the agency's ability to require foreign establishments to allow the agency to inspect their facilities.[18] For example, while inspecting establishments in

China during the heparin crisis, Chinese crude heparin consolidators refused to provide FDA full access during inspections—in particular, one consolidator refused to let FDA inspectors walk through its laboratory and refused FDA access to its records. As a result, FDA officials said they focused on the manufacturers' responsibilities to ensure that these establishments could trace their crude heparin back to qualified suppliers that produce an uncontaminated product and requested that manufacturers conduct their own investigations of any heparin products for which they received complaints or that did not meet specifications. Furthermore, FDA faces other challenges conducting foreign inspections, such as logistical issues that necessitate the agency notifying the manufacturer of the agency's intention to inspect the establishment in advance. In contrast to domestic inspections which are conducted without prior notice, FDA contacts foreign manufacturers prior to inspection to ensure that the appropriate personnel are present and that the establishment is manufacturing its product during the time of the inspection. In some cases, FDA must obtain permission from the foreign government of the country in which an establishment is located in order to conduct an inspection. FDA officials report that inspections may be conducted several months after an establishment has been notified of FDA's intent to conduct an inspection due to the need to obtain visas and other delays. As a result of such advance notice, FDA staff conducting inspections may not observe an accurate picture of the manufacturer's day-to-day operations.

FDA Lacks Complete Information on Foreign Drug Establishments

Our previous reports indicated that FDA has experienced challenges maintaining complete information on foreign drug manufacturing establishments. This lack of information, which is critical to understanding the supply chain, hampers the agency's ability to inspect foreign establishments. In 2008, we reported that FDA did not maintain a list of foreign drug establishments subject to inspection, but rather the agency relied on information from their drug establishment registration and import databases to help select establishments for inspection.[19] However, we found that these databases contained incorrect information about foreign establishments and did not contain an accurate count of foreign establishments manufacturing drugs for the U.S. market. For example, in our 2008 report, we identified that for fiscal year 2007, FDA's registration database contained information on approximately 3,000 foreign drug establishments that registered with FDA to market drugs in the United States, while the import database contained information on about 6,800 foreign establishments that offered drugs for import into the United States.[20] Some of the inaccuracies in the registration database reflected the fact that, despite being registered, some foreign establishments did not actually manufacture drugs for the U.S. market.[21] Additionally, the inaccurate count of establishments in the import database was the result of unreliable manufacturer identification numbers generated by customs brokers when a drug is offered for import.[22] As a result of these inaccuracies, FDA did not know how many foreign establishments were subject to inspection. To address these inaccuracies, we recommended that FDA enforce the requirement that establishments manufacturing drugs for the U.S. market update their registration annually and establish mechanisms for verifying information provided by the establishment at the time of registration.

Since then, FDA has taken steps to address these deficiencies and improve the information it receives from both the registration and import databases, though these efforts have not yet fully addressed the concerns we raised in 2008. For example, in June 2009, FDA began requiring all drug establishments marketing their products in the United States to submit their annual registration and listing information electronically, rather than submitting the information on paper forms to be entered into the registration database. FDA indicated that, as of September 2011, the implementation of this requirement has eliminated the human error that has been associated with the transcription of information from paper forms to electronic files. As part of electronic registration, FDA has also requested the each establishment provide a unique identification number—a Dun and Bradstreet Data Universal Numbering System (D-U-N-S®) Number[23]—as a way to help avoid duplications and errors in FDA's data systems.[24] In addition, in September 2011, FDA officials reported that the agency had begun to take steps to enforce its annual registration requirement. They indicated that FDA will now conduct outreach to establishments that have not submitted an annual registration to confirm that they are no longer producing drugs for the U.S. market or to ensure they register, as required, if they are continuing to manufacture drugs for the U.S. market. They said that if an establishment does not respond to FDA's outreach, it is to be removed from the registration database. To further address concerns with the import database, FDA has an initiative underway to eliminate duplicate information by taking steps to identify and remove all duplicate drug establishment records from existing import data over the next few years.

RECENT FDA INITIATIVES TO IMPROVE OVERSIGHT OF THE SUPPLY CHAIN

Given the difficulties that FDA has faced in inspecting and obtaining information on foreign drug manufacturers, and recognizing that more inspections alone are not sufficient to meet the challenges posed by globalization, the agency has begun to explore other initiatives to improve its oversight of the drug supply chain. We reported that FDA's overseas offices had engaged in a variety of activities to help ensure the safety of imported products. These included establishing relationships with foreign regulators, industry, and U.S. agencies overseas; gathering information about regulated products to assist with decision making; and, in China and India, conducting inspections of foreign establishments.[25] Although we noted that the impact of the offices on the safety of imported products was not yet clear, FDA staff, foreign regulators, and others pointed to several immediate benefits, such as building relationships. However, they also described challenges related to some of their collaborations with domestic FDA offices and the potential for increasing demands that could lead to an unmanageable workload. We reported that FDA was in the process of long-term strategic planning for the overseas offices, but had not developed a long-term workforce plan to help ensure that it is prepared to address potential overseas office staffing challenges, such as recruiting and retaining skilled staff. We recommended that FDA enhance its strategic planning and develop a workforce plan to help recruit and retain overseas staff and FDA concurred with our recommendations. In September 2011, FDA indicated that it had developed a 2011 to 2015 strategic plan and was in the process of updating it, and it had initiated a workforce planning process.

FDA has also implemented collaborative efforts with foreign regulatory authorities to exchange information about planned inspections as well as the results of completed inspections. In December 2008, FDA, along with its counterpart regulatory authorities of the European Union and Australia, initiated a pilot program under which the three regulators share their preliminary plans for and results of inspections of API manufacturing establishments in other countries. For example, FDA could receive the results of inspections conducted by these regulatory bodies and then determine if regulatory action or a follow-up inspection is necessary. FDA contends that prospectively sharing this information could allow these regulatory bodies to more efficiently use their resources by minimizing the overlap in their inspection plans. According to agency officials, the agency had used inspection reports from the other regulators to improve its knowledge of a small number of API manufacturing establishments, most of which had not been inspected in the last 3 years, but that it was interested in inspecting due to a pending drug application.

FDA has also taken other steps to improve the information that the agency maintains on foreign establishments shipping drugs to the United States. In August 2008, FDA contracted with two external organizations to implement the Foreign Registration Verification Program. Through this program, contractors conduct site visits to verify the existence of foreign establishments that are registered with FDA and confirm that they manufacture the products that are recorded in U.S. import records.[26] According to FDA officials, establishments that are new to the U.S. market or are importing products not typically manufactured at the same establishment are considered candidates for the verification program.[27] For example, FDA officials told us about an establishment that was selected for the program because, according to agency records, it was offering for import into the United States pickles and an API—two products not normally manufactured at the same establishment. As of September 2011, the contractors had visited 142 foreign drug establishments located in Asia, Australia, Africa, Canada, and Europe, 27 of which did not appear to exist at the address provided by the establishments at the time of registration.[28] According to FDA, the agency uses the information obtained from the contractors as screening criteria to target drug products from those establishments for review at the border.[29]

FDA is also developing initiatives that would assist its oversight of products at the border. For example, FDA is in the process of establishing its Predictive Risk-based Evaluation for Dynamic Import Compliance Targeting (PREDICT) import screening system. The system is intended to automatically score each entry based on a range of risk factors and identify high-risk items for review. FDA piloted this system on seafood products in the summer of 2007. FDA determined that the system expedited the entry of lower-risk products, while identifying a higher rate of violations among products that were tested when they were offered for import. The agency planned to have the system implemented in all locations and for all FDA-regulated products by

June 2011, although its deployment has been delayed. According to FDA, full deployment of PREDICT is currently slated for December 2011.

FDA also identified statutory changes that would help improve its oversight of drugs manufactured in foreign establishments. These include authority to (1) suspend or cancel drug establishment registrations to address concerns, including inaccurate or out-of-date information; (2) require drug establishments to use a unique establishment identifier; and (3) implement a risk-based inspection process, with flexibility to determine the frequency with which both foreign and domestic establishments are inspected, in place of the current requirement that FDA inspect domestic establishments every 2 years.

CONCLUSION

Globalization has fundamentally altered the drug supply chain and created regulatory challenges for FDA. In our prior reports we identified several concerns that demonstrate the regulatory difficulties that FDA faces conducting inspections of, and maintaining accurate information about, foreign drug establishments. While inspections provide FDA with critical information, we recognize that inspections alone are not sufficient to meet all the challenges of globalization. FDA should be credited for recent actions, such as collaborating with and exchanging information on drug establishments with foreign governments, that represent important initial steps toward addressing these challenges. However, as the agency has acknowledged, there are additional steps that it still needs to take. We have previously made recommendations to address some challenges, such as poor information and planning, and the agency has identified additional authorities that could provide it with necessary enforcement tools. In light of the growing dependence upon drugs manufactured abroad and the potential for harm, FDA needs to act quickly to implement changes across a range of activities in order to better assure the safety and availability of drugs for the U.S. market.

Chairman Harkin, Ranking Member Enzi, and Members of the Committee, this concludes my prepared statement. I would be pleased to respond to any questions you may have at this time.

RELATED GAO PRODUCTS

High-Risk Series: An Update. GAO-11-278. Washington, D.C.: February 2011.

Food and Drug Administration: Response to Heparin Contamination Helped Protect Public Health; Controls That Were Needed for Working With External Entities Were Recently Added. GAO-11-95. Washington, D.C.: October 29, 2010.

Drug Safety: FDA Has Conducted More Foreign Inspections and Begun to Improve Its Information on Foreign Establishments, but More Progress Is Needed. GAO-10-961. Washington, D.C: September 30, 2010.

Food and Drug Administration: Overseas Offices Have Taken Steps to Help Ensure Import Safety, but More Long-term Planning Is Needed. GAO-10-960. Washington, D.C.: September 30, 2010.

Food and Drug Administration: FDA Faces Challenges Meeting Its Growing Medical Product Responsibilities and Should Develop Complete Estimates of Its Resource Needs. GAO-09-581. Washington, D.C.: June 19, 2009.

High-Risk Series: An Update. GAO-09-271. Washington, D.C.: January 2009.

Drug Safety: Better Data Management and More Inspections Are Needed to Strengthen FDA's Foreign Drug Inspection Program. GAO-08-970. Washington, D.C.: September 22, 2008.

Medical Devices: FDA Faces Challenges in Conducting Inspections of Foreign Manufacturing Establishments. GAO-08-780T. Washington, D.C.: May 14, 2008.

Drug Safety: Preliminary Findings Suggest Recent FDA Initiatives Have Potential, but Do Not Fully Address Weaknesses in Its Foreign Drug Inspection Program. GAO-08-701T. Washington, D.C.: April 22, 2008.

Medical Devices: Challenges for FDA in Conducting Manufacturer Inspections. GAO-08-428T. Washington, D.C.: January 29, 2008.

Drug Safety: Preliminary Findings Suggest Weaknesses in FDA's Program for Inspecting Foreign Drug Manufacturers. GAO-08-224T. Washington, D.C.: November 1, 2007.

Food and Drug Administration: Improvements Needed in the Foreign Drug Inspection Program. GAO/HEHS-98-21. Washington, D.C.: March 17, 1998.

End Notes

[1] Drugs are defined to include, among other things, articles intended for use in the diagnosis, cure, mitigation, treatment, or prevention of disease, and include components of those articles. 21 U.S.C. § 321(g)(1)(B), (D).

[2] FDA regulations define manufacturing to include the manufacture, preparation, propagation, compounding, or processing of a drug. 21 C.F.R. § 207.3(a)(8) (2011). In addition, FDA regulations define an establishment as a place of business under one management at one general physical location. 21 C.F.R. § 207.3(a)(7) (2011). Drug manufacturers may have more than one establishment.

[3] An API includes any component of a drug that is intended to provide pharmacological activity or other direct effect in the diagnosis, cure, mitigation, treatment, or prevention of disease. See 21 C.F.R. § 210.3(b)(7) (2011). In this statement, we refer both to drug products—drugs in their finished dosage form—and to APIs as "drugs."

[4] The heparin supply chain starts with a raw source material, primarily derived from the intestines of pigs, that is processed into crude heparin. Thousands of small pig farms in Chinese villages extract and process pig intestines in small workshops called casing facilities. Consolidators collect different batches of heparin from various workshops and sell these batches to manufacturers, who further refine the crude heparin into heparin API, the active ingredient used in heparin drug products and heparin containing devices. More than half of the finished heparin products in the United States and globally are made from Chinese-sourced materials.

[5] See the Related GAO Products page at the end of this statement.

[6] GAO, High-Risk Series: An Update, GAO-11-278 (Washington, D.C.: February 2011). We first added FDA's oversight of medical products to our High-Risk Series in January 2009.

[7] In late 2008 and early 2009, FDA established overseas offices comprised of staff covering particular countries or regions. FDA has staff located overseas in Beijing, Shanghai, and Guangzhou, China; New Delhi and Mumbai, India; San Jose, Costa Rica; Mexico City, Mexico; and Santiago, Chile. In June 2011, FDA also located staff in Amman, Jordan and Pretoria, South Africa.

[8] GAO, Drug Safety: Better Data Management and More Inspections Are Needed to Strengthen FDA's Foreign Drug Inspection Program, GAO-08-970 (Washington, D.C.: Sept. 22, 2008); GAO, Food and Drug Administration: Overseas Offices Have Taken Steps to Help Ensure Import Safety, but More Long-Term Planning Is Needed, GAO-10-960 (Washington, D.C.: Sept. 30, 2010); GAO, Drug Safety: FDA Has Conducted More Foreign Inspections and Begun to Improve Its Information on Foreign Establishments, but More Progress Is Needed, GAO-10-961 (Washington, D.C.: Sept. 30, 2010); and GAO, Food and Drug Administration: Response to Heparin Contamination Helped Protect Public Health; Controls That Were Needed for Working With External Entities Were Recently Added, GAO-11-95 (Washington, D.C.: Oct. 29, 2010).

[9] Domestic and foreign establishments that manufacture drugs for the U.S. market are required to register annually with FDA. 21 U.S.C. § 360(b), (i)(1).

[10] FDA's import database contains information on drugs and other FDA-regulated products offered for entry into the United States, including information on the establishment that manufactured the drug.

[11] GMPs provide a framework for a manufacturer to follow to produce safe, pure, and high-quality drugs. See 21 C.F.R. pts. 210, 211 (2011). See also International Conference on Harmonisation of Technical Requirements for Registration of Pharmaceuticals for Human

Use, ICH Harmonised Tripartite Guideline: Good Manufacturing Practice Guide for Active Pharmaceutical Ingredients Q7 (Geneva, Switzerland: Nov. 10, 2000).

[12] See 21 U.S.C. § 360(h), (i)(3).

[13] See 21 U.S.C. § 381(a).

[14] FDA attributes this increase in fiscal year 2009 foreign drug inspections to staffing changes—the creation of a drug inspection cadre and the placement of investigators overseas—and increased resources dedicated to these types of inspections.

[15] See GAO-08-970.

[16] We noted in our September 2010 report that, in response to our inquiries and those of congressional staff, FDA had undertaken a review to determine the appropriate inspection frequency for foreign and domestic drug establishments. However, as of September 2011, this review had not been completed.

[17] For example, in the case of the heparin supply chain, the source material is primarily derived from the intestines of pigs, which is processed into the crude heparin that is refined into heparin API.

[18] See GAO-08-970.

[19] See GAO-08-970.

[20] In our 2010 report, we indicated that, in fiscal year 2009, FDA's import database contained information for about 7,000 foreign establishments, compared with the approximately 3,200 foreign drug establishments that were registered with FDA in that year. See GAO-10-961.

[21] Such establishments may have gone out of business, but not informed FDA, or the establishments may not actually ship drugs to the United States. Some foreign establishments may register with FDA, but never ship drugs to the United States. FDA officials told us that such foreign establishments may register because, in foreign markets, registration may erroneously convey an "approval" or endorsement by FDA.

[22] As we reported in 2010, the algorithm used by customs brokers to assign the manufacturer identification number does not provide for a number that is reliably reproduced or inherently unique. Consequently, according to FDA officials, multiple records may be created for a single establishment, resulting in an inflated count of the number of establishments. See GAO-10-961.

[23] The D-U-N-S® Number is a unique nine-digit sequence recognized as the federal government's universal standard for identifying and keeping track of business entities. Submitting the site-specific number for an entity would provide, by reference to the number, certain business information for that entity that is otherwise required for drug establishment registration.

[24] Additionally, FDA, in conjunction with 20 of the nearly 50 federal agencies involved in the oversight of products imported into the United States, supports efforts for Customs and Border Protection—which control the implementation of this proposal—to adopt unique establishment identifiers for all establishments whose products, including drugs, are imported into the United States.

[25] We also reported that FDA overseas officials had started to provide training, responses to queries, and other assistance to foreign stakeholders to help them improve their regulatory systems and better understand FDA regulations.

[26] According to FDA officials, the Foreign Registration Verification Program covers establishments manufacturing all FDA-regulated products.

[27] To select establishments for the Foreign Registration Verification Program, FDA uses information from its import database to determine the products that establishments are

shipping to the United States and to identify establishments that are importing a variety of products.

[28] According to FDA, the agency has engaged contractors to conduct at least 125 more such visits of foreign drug manufacturing establishments during the coming year.

[29] In our 2010 report, we noted that FDA had taken action against 2 of the establishments that appeared not to exist by deactivating their registration and alerting FDA import staff so that they could detain any products offered for import by these establishments, thus preventing these products from being imported into the United States.

INDEX

A

abuse, 8
access, 2, 18, 36, 38, 39, 51, 84
accountability, 2, 4, 16, 19, 20, 31, 75
accounting, 8, 80
accounting standards, 8
accreditation, 2, 15, 18, 25, 61
acetaminophen, 28
acid, 68
ADR, 5, 9
adults, 68
adverse effects, 20
adverse event, 17, 69, 80
Africa, 87
agencies, 11, 65, 70, 74, 86, 91
AIDS, 56, 65
algorithm, 91
anticoagulant, 71
antidepressants, 69
Argentina, 46
Asia, 87
aspartate, 28
assessment, 36, 61, 70
asthma, 54
audit(s), 81
authentication, 2, 10, 17, 29, 40, 41, 55
authenticity, 31, 47
authorities, 8, 30, 41, 42, 68, 69, 70, 72, 73, 75, 81, 86, 88
authority, 11, 17, 29, 30, 62, 65, 72, 73, 74, 88
awareness, 49, 52

B

background information, 21
barriers, 39
Beijing, 70, 90
Belgium, 70
benefits, 17, 18, 36, 86
black market, 55
blood, 28, 69, 80
blood clot, 80
Brazil, 46, 55
browser, 64
building blocks, 41
business model, 50

C

calcium, 28
cancer, 5, 28, 56, 63
candidates, 87
carbamazepine, 28
case study, 71
CDC, 5
certification, 73
CFR, 5, 10, 21, 22, 23, 26
chain of distribution, 40

chain pharmacies, vii, 1, 56
challenges, 31, 35, 51, 64, 65, 68, 70, 72, 75, 77, 78, 79, 80, 81, 83, 84, 86, 88
chemical, vii, 1, 3, 68, 71, 72
chemotherapy, 69
children, 68
Chile, 70, 90
China, 46, 55, 68, 70, 71, 80, 81, 84, 86, 90
cholesterol, 28, 69
chondroitin sulfate, 71
citizens, 46, 55, 66
City, 57, 70, 90
collaboration, 58, 69
commerce, 11, 36, 73, 74
commercial, 11, 18, 45
communication, 20, 52
communication systems, 20
community, vii, 1, 5, 49, 50, 51, 52
compatibility, 14
complement, 30
complexity, 68, 77, 80
compliance, 10, 15, 18, 19, 21, 51, 73, 82
complications, 11
compression, 65
confidentiality, 2, 18
congress, vii, viii, 1, 2, 3, 4, 8, 10, 11, 14, 15, 16, 20, 21, 22, 24, 25, 26, 34, 35, 36, 38, 40, 47, 56, 57
congressional hearings, 14
connectivity, 42
consensus, 10, 34, 41, 43, 51, 52
consulting, 55
consumers, vii, 1, 3, 4, 5, 27, 28, 37, 38, 39, 52, 62, 63, 64, 68, 69, 71, 72, 73, 74, 75
containers, 14
contaminant, 18, 68, 71
contamination, 3, 31, 68, 71, 80
controlled substances, 28
coordination, 70
copyright, 21
corruption, 63
cost, 2, 11, 16, 19, 39, 41, 42, 51, 54, 64, 69, 75
Costa Rica, 70, 90
cough, 68
counterfeit product, vii, 1, 50
counterfeiting, 3, 11, 16, 18, 31, 39, 42, 50, 68, 74
covering, 90
criminals, 42, 54, 56, 68, 71, 72, 74
cure, 90
customers, 9
Customs and Border Protection, 91

D

danger, 28, 80
data collection, 2
data communication, 26
database, 11, 17, 81, 85, 90, 91
deaths, 68, 71, 80
deficiencies, 79, 85
deficit, 28
Department of Health and Human Services, 3, 20, 22, 26, 27, 67
Department of Justice, 20, 21
destruction, 73
detection, 54, 70
detention, 74
developing countries, 64
diabetes, 28
diodes, 64
diseases, 47
disorder, 28
dispenser, vii, 1, 2, 5, 6, 14, 15, 17, 55
distribution, vii, 1, 3, 4, 5, 8, 9, 10, 14, 17, 19, 24, 28, 29, 31, 34, 38, 39, 41, 42, 46, 47, 51, 53, 54, 55, 56, 62, 63, 68, 75
DNA, 64
DNA testing, 64
dosage, vii, 1, 16, 90
draft, 15, 24, 25, 35, 41, 42, 57
drug package, vii, 1, 17, 30, 54
drug safety, 4, 5, 38, 75
drugs, vii, 1, 2, 3, 4, 5, 8, 9, 10, 11, 14, 16, 18, 20, 21, 22, 28, 29, 30, 31, 36, 40, 42, 46, 49, 50, 53, 54, 55, 56, 58, 62, 63, 67, 68, 69, 71, 72, 73, 74, 77, 79, 80, 81, 82, 83, 84, 85, 87, 88, 90, 91

E

eBay, 64
e-commerce, 64
economic development, 70
editors, 21, 25
employees, 49
encryption, 11
energy, 65
enforcement, 9, 11, 19, 42, 88
England, 70
environment, 69, 80
EU, 58
Europe, 87
European Parliament, 58
European Union, 46, 58, 86
evidence, 72, 81, 82
expertise, 62, 70
export market, 70
exports, 8

F

factories, 8
farms, 90
fear, 69
federal agency, 18
federal authorities, 52, 63
federal government, 91
federal law, vii, viii, 2, 4, 14, 54
Federal Register, 23, 62
fever, 68
fillers, 6, 11
financial, 2, 50
financial resources, 50
fiscal year 2009, 78, 83, 91
flexibility, 79, 88
food, 68, 69
Food and Drug Administration, 2, 3, 5, 10, 11, 20, 21, 22, 24, 26, 27, 29, 30, 40, 42, 58, 65, 67, 77, 78, 79, 89, 90
force, 59
formula, 68, 73
fraud, 40, 55

G

GAO, 21, 77, 78, 79, 89, 90, 91
generic drugs, 37, 38, 39
Georgia, 56
globalization, 70, 72, 75, 79, 80, 86, 88
globalized marketplace, 75
glucose, 28, 69
glycerin, 68
glycol, 68
goods and services, 37
governments, 11, 70, 74, 88
GPS, 64
growth, 4, 55, 56, 80
growth hormone, 4, 55, 56
Guangzhou, 70, 90
guidance, 10, 18, 22, 29, 47
guidelines, 8, 9, 11, 34

H

Haiti, 68
health, vii, viii, 1, 4, 5, 11, 16, 25, 28, 37, 38, 50, 61, 69, 70, 73, 74, 75
Health and Human Services, 3, 22
health care, vii, viii, 1, 4, 5, 16, 37
health care system, 37
health risks, 73
HHS, 3, 23, 27, 67
history, 16, 17, 19, 23, 29, 31, 36, 39, 56
HIV, 54
hormone, 4
hospital pharmacist, vii, 1
House, 2, 3, 15, 20, 22, 24, 25, 26, 27, 33, 37, 39, 41, 42, 45, 46, 49, 52, 53, 61, 63
House of Representatives, 20, 26
human, 4, 21, 46, 52, 56, 64, 85
human genome, 64

I

identification, 10, 11, 14, 18, 29, 40, 41, 46, 72, 75, 85, 91
imported products, 68, 79, 86

imports, 8, 67, 69, 75
imprisonment, 11
improvements, 34, 52
India, 46, 70, 80, 81, 86, 90
individuals, 54
industries, 16
industry, viii, 3, 4, 5, 8, 9, 14, 16, 20, 29, 34, 35, 37, 38, 39, 41, 42, 53, 55, 57, 58, 62, 63, 65, 68, 69, 70, 71, 72, 73, 74, 77, 80, 86
information sharing, 69
information technology, 46
infrastructure, 42
ingredients, 3, 6, 17, 21, 28, 67, 68, 72
inspections, 11, 70, 71, 73, 77, 78, 79, 80, 82, 83, 86, 88, 91
inspectors, 84
insulin, 4, 28, 56, 58, 69
integrity, viii, 3, 4, 8, 25, 30, 31, 38, 39, 47, 52, 61, 63, 64, 65, 69, 72, 75
interface, 65
international standards, 47, 71
interoperability, 41, 42
investments, 54
issues, vii, viii, 4, 13, 42, 51, 61, 62, 78, 84
Italy, 55, 70

J

Jordan, 70, 90
jurisdiction, 19

L

labeling, 2, 17, 18, 42
landscape, 46, 67
laparoscopy, 64
laptop, 64
Latin America, 81
law enforcement, 56
laws, 2, 11, 13, 24, 34, 35, 41, 46, 50, 54, 82
laws and regulations, 11, 82
lead, 3, 28, 39, 68, 75, 86
leadership, 2, 19, 20, 33, 34, 35
legislation, 2, 11, 14, 15, 16, 17, 18, 19, 20, 34, 40, 45, 46, 47, 57, 58, 62, 64, 75
legislative proposals, 15, 18, 19, 30
light, 79, 88
litigation, 10
logistics, 5, 6, 16, 38

M

majority, 2, 20, 40, 83
management, 18, 20, 73, 90
manufacturing, 2, 3, 4, 10, 11, 16, 17, 28, 30, 40, 67, 69, 71, 72, 75, 77, 78, 79, 80, 81, 82, 83, 84, 86, 90, 91, 92
mapping, 64
marketing, 18, 80, 85
marketplace, 68
materials, 3, 6, 24, 27, 68, 73, 90
matrix, 52
media, 63
Medicaid, 4, 54, 57
medical, vii, 1, 4, 14, 28, 53, 67, 68, 69, 73, 74, 80, 90
medication, 6, 28, 50, 68, 80
medicine, 28, 35, 36, 39, 41, 46, 56, 63, 68
membership, 38
memory, 65
methodology, 71
Mexico, 70, 90
migration, 36
mission, 34, 38, 47, 70
modifications, 62
momentum, 64
MRI, 64

N

nanotechnology, 11
networking, 65
Nigeria, 68
normal distribution, 50

O

officials, 78, 79, 81, 83, 84, 85, 87, 91
operations, 15, 39, 84
opportunities, 2, 3, 27, 68, 70, 72
outreach, 85
overlap, 87
oversight, 8, 19, 62, 63, 78, 79, 80, 81, 82, 86, 87, 88, 90, 91
ownership, 5, 16, 63

P

pain, 28
Panama, 68
participants, 14, 17, 18, 19, 40, 47, 50, 51, 65
pedigree, 2, 8, 9, 14, 16, 23, 24, 33, 34, 35, 36, 39, 46, 50, 51, 54
penalties, 8, 9, 11, 18, 74
permission, 84
permit, 11, 73, 74
pharmaceutical(s), vii, viii, 2, 4, 5, 6, 8, 9, 10, 15, 16, 22, 23, 30, 33, 34, 37, 38, 39, 40, 42, 46, 47, 49, 50, 51, 54, 56, 58, 67, 77, 80
physicians, vii, 1, 5, 29, 50
pigs, 71, 90, 91
plants, 65, 71
playing, 72, 73, 74
policy, 10, 16, 25, 38, 47, 50
policy makers, 50
policymakers, 2, 14, 16
population, 71
preparation, 90
prescription drugs, vii, 1, 4, 29, 33, 35, 36, 40, 50, 52, 54, 69
president, v, viii, 30, 62, 67
prevention, 75, 90
principles, 39, 53
private sector, 47
probability, 11
producers, 8
profit, 29, 42, 50
profit margin, 50
project, 26
propagation, 90
protection, 25, 30, 47, 62
public health, 17, 25, 28, 30, 31, 34, 38, 42, 53, 57, 61, 68, 69
public policy, 53
public safety, 66
publishing, 41
purity, 82

Q

quality control, 11, 69, 72
quality improvement, 42

R

Radiation, 57
radio, 18
raw materials, 11, 72
recall, 17, 19, 29, 72, 73
recommendations, 16, 63, 86, 88
recovery, 56
recruiting, 86
recycling, 54
regulations, 5, 9, 11, 18, 24, 42, 46, 47, 58, 79, 82, 90, 91
regulatory agencies, 74
regulatory bodies, 87
regulatory requirements, 10
regulatory systems, 67, 91
repackaging, 10, 17, 40
reputation, 2, 16
requirements, 2, 10, 11, 14, 15, 16, 17, 19, 22, 23, 30, 34, 35, 36, 39, 40, 42, 51, 62, 64, 73, 82
resale, 7, 16
resolution, 75
resources, 65, 69, 70, 71, 74, 87, 91
response, 19, 30, 50, 91
retail, 3, 5, 9, 11, 17, 20, 25, 56, 58, 62
revenue, 5

risk(s), 3, 11, 28, 29, 46, 53, 54, 56, 57, 68, 69, 70, 71, 72, 73, 74, 79, 87, 88
risk factors, 11, 87
rules, 35

S

safety, 4, 8, 11, 21, 22, 28, 30, 33, 34, 35, 36, 39, 41, 42, 47, 50, 51, 52, 54, 61, 67, 68, 69, 70, 72, 74, 75, 77, 79, 80, 82, 86, 88
savings, 34, 38
schizophrenia, 54
science, 69
scope, 16, 19, 65
seafood, 87
security, viii, 2, 4, 5, 8, 10, 11, 13, 14, 15, 16, 17, 19, 23, 30, 31, 38, 40, 41, 42, 47, 50, 51, 55, 57, 69, 72, 74, 75
security threats, 11
seizure, 4
seller, 14
Senate, 2, 15, 20, 22, 24, 25, 26, 30, 34, 39, 43, 52, 63, 67, 77
September 11, 58
sequencing, 64
services, 64
short supply, 34
shortage, 55, 63
side effects, 28
software, 5, 64
solution, 36, 39, 47, 50, 57, 63, 65
South Africa, 70, 90
specifications, 84
spending, 37
spreadsheets, 64
staffing, 86, 91
stakeholder groups, 11
stakeholders, viii, 4, 11, 14, 16, 20, 29, 30, 31, 34, 35, 36, 38, 47, 51, 52, 53, 64, 79, 91
state(s), viii, 2, 4, 5, 8, 9, 11, 13, 14, 15, 16, 18, 19, 20, 24, 34, 35, 36, 40, 41, 42, 46, 47, 50, 52, 51, 54, 56, 61, 62, 63, 64, 65, 66
state laws, 2, 5, 42, 54
state legislatures, 2
statutes, 16, 24
statutory authority, 19, 73
statutory provisions, 74
sterile, 29
stock, 19, 29
storage, vii, 1, 3, 8, 9, 11, 16, 28, 29, 58, 68
strategic planning, 86
structure, 56
substitution, vii, 1
succession, 55
suppliers, 4, 11, 37, 74, 84
surveillance, 70, 71
sustainability, 38
Switzerland, 91

T

target, 50, 87
Task Force, 21
taxpayers, 64
technical assistance, 30
technological advancement, 55
technologies, 2, 10, 14, 17, 42, 51, 52
technology, 5, 11, 15, 19, 20, 39, 40, 42, 54
testing, 71, 72
theft, 6, 11, 16, 56, 68, 74
therapy, 28
threats, 30, 42, 68, 73, 74, 75
time frame, 18, 31, 54
tissue, 71
Title I, 20
Title II, 20
Title V, 11, 24
tobacco, 11
tracks, 55
trade, 2, 8, 9
trading partners, 49
trafficking, 11
training, 50, 70, 79, 91
transactions, 17, 47, 50
transcription, 85
transparency, 31, 75
transport, vii, 1, 5, 6

transportation, 3, 16, 67
treatment, 35, 65, 90
Turkey, 46, 55

U

unacceptable risk, 62
uniform, 14, 19, 34, 36, 39, 40, 42, 47, 51, 52, 64
United Kingdom, 4, 21
United States, 3, 4, 5, 11, 20, 21, 22, 28, 29, 30, 37, 38, 49, 50, 52, 57, 58, 62, 67, 68, 69, 71, 72, 73, 74, 77, 80, 81, 82, 83, 85, 87, 90, 91, 92
updating, 86
up-front costs, 17
USA, 58

V

validation, 10, 11, 29, 40
variations, 35
Viagra, 50
Vice President, v, viii, 24, 33, 37, 45
vocabulary, 25

W

Washington, 21, 22, 25, 89, 90
web, 55, 62
wholesale, vii, 1, 2, 5, 6, 8, 9, 10, 15, 19, 24, 38, 42, 50, 62, 63, 65
wind turbines, 65
workforce, 79, 81, 86
working groups, 35
workload, 86
worldwide, 68, 70